DEATH
OF A
DREAM

*One Family's
Experience of the
1862 US/Dakota War*

*Honoring my ancestors
Telling their story
For you.*

Paul Lundborg

Paul Lundborg

1st edition, January 2013

For permission to copy or share this work, please write:

Paul Lundborg
1824 – 27th Ave NW
Olympia, WA 98502-3914
Email: prlundborg@comcast.net

Ordering Information at www.createspace.com/4177474
or at www.amazon.com

ISBN-13: 978-1482578102
ISBN-10: 1482578107

Cover original artwork by Susan Volkmann of Wenatchee, WA.
Book design by Mary Helgesen Gabel, Gabel Graphics. www.gabelgraphics.com
Heading font is Brioso Pro
Text font is Berthold Baskerville
Ornaments are Linotype Decoration Pi
Cover font is Berthold Walbaum Book

Author

Paul Lundborg grew up in Milan, Minnesota. He is a graduate of Augustana College in Sioux Falls, South Dakota, and Luther Theological Seminary in St. Paul, Minnesota. In 2006 he retired after 37 years as a pastor of the Evangelical Lutheran Church in America. He is a great, great grandson of Swedish farmers who settled in Minnesota in 1861 as part of an extended family numbering 21 persons.

The author has written a family legacy book. The story concerns his family—Swedish ancestors who came to America in 1861 with dreams of a new beginning. Unfortunately, 13 members of this extended family of 21 were victims of a cruel attack by Indians in the US/Dakota War of 1862. Even if you aren't related to the author, you might appreciate this very real story of ordinary people shockingly caught up in the powerful forces of manifest destiny and cross-cultural warfare. The story of what took place on August 20, 1862, the third day of a six-week war that left a permanent imprint on thousands of individual lives and all of Minnesota state history, is the heart of this book. Skip the genealogy if you wish, but know that such data roots the family in a very particular place at a very particular time.

Telling this story in 2012, 150 years after the events happened, is done to commemorate the lives of the author's family and express gratitude for the lives of the eight survivors whose descendants are now many. And the story is told not to awaken dated interracial anger but to shed light on the lives of regular people trying to cope with and make sense of difficult times.

I wish to express my gratitude to artist Susan Volkmann for her creativity in preparing the original cover art and to my editor and book designer, Mary Gabel.

Dedication

≈

In the cemetery of Peace Lutheran Church in New London, Minnesota, stands a monument to the 13 victims of the Monson Lake Massacre of August 20, 1862. All were part of a large extended family of 21 Lundborgs and Brobergs who farmed as neighbors in rural Västergötland, Sweden, near the community of Vårgårda and emigrated to settle together in Minnesota in 1861.

Death of a Dream *is a living monument—not stone, but words forming a story—I dedicate to the survivors of that massacre. They have been gone for many years, but their story has come to light again in 2012, the sesquicentennial year of the tragic US/Dakota War. This brief war cost many lives, revealed a huge cultural division between the Dakota people and the immigrant settlers, and scarred surviving generations on both sides.*

First and foremost, I honor my great, great grandparents Andreas and Lena Lundborg. In their early 50's, they escaped death that day and led six surviving family members on a journey to safety that would take them many miles and several months.

The remaining survivors were their children Johannes (29) and his wife Kristina (18) who was eight months pregnant, Johanna (13) and Samuel (9), plus two others—16-year-old Anna Stina Broberg and her 7-year-old cousin Peter orphaned by the deaths of their parents.

Their dream of a new beginning in America became a nightmare of grief. We who are their descendants are thankful for their courage, sacrifice, and persistence through those difficult days and years. They survived, we live, and we are deeply touched by their story.

Learning the story of my ancestors has renewed my appreciation for my family roots and has caused me to be ever more deeply grateful for my immediate family: my beloved wife, Rose Ann, and our sons, their wives, and daughters. Thanks be to God. All of us, heirs together of the grace of life.

Paul S. Lundborg
October 8, 2012

Table of Contents

೧೧

Preface

༄༅

In 1981, at the age of 38, I learned from one of my father's sisters that three of my great grandfather's brothers were killed in the US/Dakota War of 1862. The power of those few details was magnified considerably because the story entered an empty spot in my life. Other than being able to say, "My dad's relatives came from Sweden, and my mom's relatives came from Norway," I was speechless concerning matters of genealogy and family history. Maybe if I had first learned something less dramatic, like "My dad's grandfather's name was Johannes," the learning curve would have been slow and gradual. But my first learning on that day in 1981 was that my dad's grandfather's brothers died violent deaths at the hands of a few Dakota Indians four years into Minnesota's emerging statehood in the early days of the Civil War. Wow! My aunt's matter-of-fact recounting of this story caused me to remember hearing about what was called "The Sioux Uprising of 1862" in the 6th grade while studying Minnesota state history. And my mind quickly leapt into interpretive mode, and I heard myself say aloud, " If my great grandfather had also been killed, I wouldn't be here!" My historical awareness was instantly intensified by a deeply felt personal connection. I love life! I'm in my late 30's! I'm a husband and a father of two sons! I might never have been born! My mortality was jolted into a new level of self-awareness.

A secondary realization was this violent episode happened very near my hometown—Milan, Minnesota—where I spent my first 18 years. It took place near Sunburg. I knew of Sunburg. At least I had heard of it. In fact, I thought to myself as I tried to picture Sunburg on a map, "Isn't Sunburg close to Milan?" Why had I never heard this story before? Growing up 50 miles away from the place where an event of epic family proportions happened, how could it be that no one told me this story? Or had someone told me and I didn't remember? I felt clueless, and I was mad either at my own ignorance or at everyone else for failing to inform me of this family connection to such significant history.

In those days I just happened to be enamored by Native American history, culture, and religion. I had just finished reading the novel, *Hanta-Yo,* 800+ pages of a mystical history of the Dakota people. Along with two friends who read the same book I was helping to build a tipi in the way of the Dakota tribe. Yes, I'm a bit of a romantic, and I was infatuated by what I was learning of their culture. What a time to learn that these people had brutally killed members of my family! I was reeling with momentary consciousness of my own non-existence, feeling left out and angry because I had never heard this story earlier, and now I was disillusioned by my naïve, idealistic image of the noble savage.

I tell this to attempt to convey the power this story carried when I first heard it in my 38th year. Since that time I have retired (2006), traveled the length of the Minnesota River viewing the sites of the 1862 war and stopped in nearly every library, museum, and historical society; traveled several times to Sweden to see the homeland and meet relatives; and read many books and talked to even more people. Now in my 69th year the story still speaks to me, and I want to share this version of the story first with my family and then with others who might be interested.

By this time I've realized what originally was a family story impacting me is far more. It is a profound human story of parents and children, worry, dreams, fears, warfare, suffering, and courage that speaks a universal message. My family members experienced in a dramatic way during an explosive time in United States' history what many people have known throughout the centuries. I want others to hear this family story, and that is why I write.

A story's content is always shaped by the story teller, and I've read and heard many versions of my family's story that differ over the details. As you compare and contrast what you are about to read with some other versions, please don't allow any variable particulars obscure the grit, courage and suffering revealed in the lives of my ancestors.

In 2012, the year of the 150th anniversary of the Dakota/ US War of 1862, I hope the story of my family members who suffered and died through that tragedy might be told in such a way that their memory is honored and we who follow after them express our deep gratitude for their willingness to follow their dream. I hope all who come to know this story more fully will eventually come to terms with the grief and anger it initially evokes and become more willing to see the same grief and anger among the descendants of the Dakota people, whose families also understand the death of a dream. And finally, I hope all will understand our own hurts well enough to set them aside and take up the important work of acknowledging the common humanity of all persons of all races. For we are all related.

Paul Lundborg
Olympia, Washington
July 10, 2012

Chapter One

∽

Introducing the Story
The Time, the Place, the People

I want to tell you a story about my family, and I want to tell it slowly and carefully. It's an exciting story, an important story, very dramatic, and it's true. The essential family story I want to tell took place on a specific day, August 20 in 1862. And it happened in a very specific place in what was then known as Monongalia County in Minnesota. It's now known as Kandiyohi County right near the border with Swift County, and the site is now the location of Monson Lake State Park a few miles from Sunburg, the closest town. Those details are important because they are part of the context of the story, and I think you'll find it helpful to learn more of this story's background.

I'm writing about the Lundborgs, my dad's side of my family. As a child I never heard this story. I knew my father's family mostly through an annual family reunion held at the farm near Cokato. After dad's death when I was 10, we didn't attend many other reunions. Looking back, I remember the music, the big picnic, Grandma Lundborg's long table prayer, playing softball against the grownups, and making music. If story telling happened at those reunions, I never knew it. I never heard THE story.

The story is tragic, so you might wonder why I place a high value on it. My only explanation is that the magnitude of the family tragedy and its intersection with Minnesota's emerging statehood in 1858, the Civil War (1861–65), and the waves of immigrants beginning to settle America in the mid-19th century serve to locate my ancestors in a most unique place and time. This story conveys American history in a way that a textbook in school could never do. It's a story that makes history become personal. It's about my family.

The basic story is this: *On August 20, 1862, thirteen Swedish immigrant settlers were killed in the US/Dakota War on a plot of ground near present day Sunburg, Minnesota. The dead included three young men with the surname of Lundborg and ten members of a family named Broberg. All of these people were related to each other and had deep roots in the same area of Sweden before their recent arrival in America. In July 1861 they settled as four households within two miles of each other. They were my relatives. I want to tell you about these four households, those who died, and those who survived.*

Household #1

Andreas (50) and wife Maja Lena (51) Lundborg, my great, great grandparents, survived. They are the patriarch and matriarch of these family units, and I will refer to them as Andreas and Lena. Their sons Anders (25), Gustaf (23), and Lars (21) were all killed that August day. Little brother Samuel (9) was seriously wounded but survived, and his 13-year-old sister, Johanna, was not harmed. Daughter Sarah (19) was not present. She was already married, had one child and was pregnant with the next, and did not come to America with them. She remained with her husband, Johannes Lundquist, back in the homeland.

Household #2

Johannes (29) and Kristina (18) Lundborg, my great grand-parents, survived. They were married in November of 1861, and by August 20, 1862 Kristina was eight months pregnant.

I am guessing who lived where as I name the specific residents of each of the Lundborg cabins. But the records indicate Andreas filed a claim for land on section 5 and Johannes filed for section 6 in Arctander Township, and it is difficult to imagine all nine family members living in one cabin. Perhaps they did, but it's difficult to imagine. Oral tradition adds a new wrinkle by saying that in July of 1862 new immigrants from Sweden—the Swenson family—arrived and moved in with Andreas and Lena.

Household #3

The Broberg cabins were about two miles away from the Lundborgs. Anders (42)—most often called A.P.—and his wife Christina (36) Broberg were both killed. Their children Johannes (13), Andreas (10), and Christina (7) were killed, but daughter Anna Stina (16) survived. Also killed was Johannes Nilsson (about 21), a half brother to Christina Broberg. He was known as Uncle John, and he had arrived from Sweden in July, one month earlier. He served as their child care and field work assistant.

Household #4

A. P.'s younger brother, Daniel (38) and wife Anna Stina (30) Broberg were killed along with their sons Alfred (4) and John (10 months). Son Andreas Peter (7), most often called Peter, survived.

Thirteen members of one extended family living in four households were dead. One was wounded. All who survived were marked with this memory forever. And again, they were my relatives.

Listening to the details of this story can easily become confusing. The dictionary of Swedish names for the era was obviously limited, so don't get anxious if you can't keep the names straight. The larger context of the story has a bottom line, and it's this. The Andreas and Lena Lundborg family in America, which numbered nine on August 19, numbered six on August 20. The A.P. and Christina Broberg family, which numbered seven, now numbered one. The Daniel and Anna Stina Broberg family was six, and also became one. The lives of 21 newcomers were reduced to eight.

Chapter Two

ɔ๏

Back to the Beginning

Here begins a brief genealogy so you can know something about the roots of these families. If history bores you, you're in trouble for a while. If you're really impatient, you can skip it, but you might be sorry. The story of August 20, 1862, is the exciting part, but here's a peek at the foundation that undergirds the story.

First Generation

Torsten Algottson (1712–?). That's where I start. He's my great, great grandfather's great grandfather. There must have been prior generations, but I don't know about them—yet. Later generations might find earlier information, but I will begin with 1712. It's the year Torsten was born, and even though his death is not recorded, the records indicate he was married and had children. These are the records found through the church of Sweden, and they tell us he was born on the Tåstorp Farm. A date for marriage is not known, but we can assume he was married to Karin Persdotter because they are the parents of four children: Lena, Britta, Peter, and Anders.

The closest major Swedish city to the Tåstorp Farm is Gothenburg, about 50 miles southwest on the west coast of

Sweden. The area that was the Tåstorp farm is located not far from present day Vårgårda in the state of Västergötland, and the next four generations in this family had their origins on the same farm.

Lundborg was not their last name in 1712. Torsten must have been the son of Algott—which is why his last name is Algottsson. Sweden's patronymic system caused his name to be Torsten Algottsson. And his son Peter was named Peter Torstenson, and he was followed by Lars Peterson, Andreas Larsson, and Johannes Andersson. These are the ancestors I claim in the line that led to my birth, so their names will be in bold print as the narrative progresses. This naming system made sense for their day, but for now it is confusing. In 1861 when Andreas Larsson left Sweden, he became Andreas Lundborg by his own choosing. Maybe he chose that name because by that time the Tåstorp Farm had become part of a larger collective known as the Lund *By* (a Swedish word referring to a number of farms that found a way to work together). But I'm getting ahead of myself. All that is known thus far about this generation is that Torsten and Karin Persdotter (she's the daughter of Per) had four children, and they lived at Tåstorp.

Second Generation

The children of Torsten and Karin were:

> Lena Torstensdotter (1732–?)
>
> Britta Torstensdotter (1734–?)
>
> **Peter Torstenson** (1735–2/17/1803) 68 years.
>
> Anders Torstenson (1742–6/8/1808) 66 years.

The question marks in the dates ascribed to Lena and Britta mean the dates of their deaths are not known to the record keepers. The death dates for the sons are known. Why not for the daughters? Did they marry and move away? Or did they die in infancy and not get recorded? The reader is free to speculate.

Third Generation

Third generation members born to **Peter Torstenson** and **Kjerstin Persdotter** numbered eight and included the following:

> Maria Pettersdotter (1763–?)
>
> Stina Pettersdotter (1766–11/19/1841) 75 years.
>
> Johannes Petterson (2/5/1770–?)
>
> Sara Pettersdotter (2/10/1774–5/11/1774) 3 months.
>
> Sara Pettersdotter (5/4/1775–?)
>
> Pehr Petterson (5/14/1778–?)
>
> Cathrina Pettersdotter (9/12/1779–?)
>
> **Lars Petterson** (6/16/1783–3/18/1825) 41 years.

Death dates are recorded only for Stina, Sara #1, and Lars. Lars is the only one with a record of marriage and children. When locations are mentioned in the records, the Tåstorp farm is specifically mentioned, as are the churches of Tumberg, Södra Härene, Kullings-Skövde, or Algutstorp which are all located close to the farm. I assume these churches were important because the families worshipped in the one closest to where they lived. Sundays, festivals of Christmas, Easter, Pentecost, plus baptisms, confirmations, weddings, funerals—the milestone events of life were celebrated here. Sweden's church records also contain significant data concerning the lives of our ancestors. Lars married **Sarah Borjesdotter** on July 14, 1805. He lived to be 41, and she died at age 40, much younger than Lars' parents who died at 57 and 68. Farm life was not easy.

I'm also including the family of Anders, Peter's brother and younger son of Torsten and Karin, in this genealogy even though I am not a direct descendant of his. Anders' descendants eventually become the Brobergs, so this generation makes the connection between the Lundborgs and the Brobergs. Children born to Anders and Stina numbered three and included the following:

Britta Andersdotter (1/10/1778–11/22/1847) 69 years. Born on the Tåstorp Farm with no record of marriage. Location of death and burial are not known.

Catrina Andersdotter *(1/27/1782–5/11/1829) 47 years. She, too, was born on the Tåstorp Farm, and she married* Andreas Danielson *(1778–1828) on June 18, 1803. They were married young—Andreas at 25 and Catrina at 21—and they both died young. She lived to 47 and he to 50. Their children included:* Johanna *(1/2/1806–6/1/1886),* Johannes *(4/27/1810–3/12/1866), and* Lars *(11/12/1815–12/23/1890). But most important to this story are their youngest children* Anders Petter *(9/16/1819–8/20/1862) and* Daniel Petter *(1/8/1824–8/20/1862)* Andreason. *When they immigrated to America in 1861, they changed their last name to* Broberg. *The reason why is not apparent anywhere. This linkage explains the* Lundborg/Broberg *relationship as more than a friendship. They were cousins—second cousins or first cousins once removed? I'm not sure. Andreas Lundborg, A. P. Broberg, and Daniel Broberg shared the same great, grandfather. And their grandfathers were brothers. They were relatives in addition to being neighbors and friends. All of this is in italics because it needs to be more obvious to the reader that this is important information.*

Bengt Andersson (12/6/1793–9/10/1846) 52 years. The youngest of Anders and Stina was also born on the Tåstorp farm. There is no record of marriage or children.

Fourth Generation

Lars and **Sarah** had five children:

Johannes Larsson (1806–1/17/1810) 4 years.

Johannes Larsson (9/15/1806–3/12/1844) 37 years.

Why two consecutive children named Johannes? This is a mystery. It could be there are mistakes in the records. Their birth date is in the same year. Could they be twins? With the same name? Unlikely. I don't know what to do with it, but it's in the records.

Andreas Andrew Larsson (2/28/1812–1/8/1891) 78 years. This is my great, great grandfather who later changed his name to Lundborg. He has an extra name. On July 7, 1832, he married Maja Lena Johansdotter (10/11/1810–10/18/1870) 60 years. They left for America in 1861 about the same time as A. P. and Daniel Andreasson (Broberg) and their wives.

Kaija Larsdotter (9/8/1815–1815) She lived and died within one year.

Caija Larsdotter (4/22/1817–11/14/1888) 71 years.

Fifth Generation

Andreas and Lena had eleven children. Since 1712 all the descendants of Torsten Algottson had been born, worked, and lived in that same Swedish countryside, but in 1858 three of Andreas and Lena's children left for America, and they would be joined in Minnesota by the rest of the family (except for daughter Sarah who remained in Sweden) in 1861. Here are their 11 children with just the bare-bones statistics. Their story will come later.

Johannes Andersson Lundborg (9/28/1832–11/15/1899) 67 years. He was the firstborn of the generation that faced the biggest changes. As the family increased in number and the available land became less, the attraction of a new land overseas grew more enticing. Johannes survived the horrors of August 20, 1862, and he is my great grandfather.

Börje Andersson (12/21/1833–1/15/1834). Lived three-and-one-half weeks. Records say he "suffocated by accident."

Börje Andersson (10/9/1835–4/3/1837. Lived 18 months. Died of measles.

Anders Petter Andersson Lundborg (4/23/1837–*8/20/1862*). Lived 25 years.

Gustaf Andersson Lundborg (4/30/1839–*8/20/1862*). Lived 23 years.

Lars Andersson Lundborg (12/22/1840–*8/20/1862*). Lived 21 years.

Sarah Andersdotter Lundquist (11/17/1842–5/26/1907). Lived 64 years.

Johanna Andersdotter (10/2/1844–12/15/1844). Lived two-and-one-half months and died of pneumonia.

Johanna Andersdotter (1/22/1846–3/16/1847). Lived one year, two months and died of pneumonia.

Johanna Andersdotter Lundborg Paulson (12/21/1848–3/21/1916). Lived 67 years.

Samuel Andersson Lundborg (2/12/1853–5/23/1920). Lived 61 years.

Why and when did this family leave Sweden?

Chapter Three

ᘒᘏ

The Decision

The day is January 1, 1858, and the place is the Tåstorp Farm in Sweden in the household of Andreas Larsson and Lena Johansdotter. The day's work is done, dinner is finished, and before anyone leaves the table Andreas announces, "We're going to America." Yes, I know the Swedes have a reputation for being terse, so I'm exaggerating a bit. He might have said more.

I'm imagining this scene because there must have been a moment in time when the monumental decision to leave home and move to a brand new country was made, but I don't know when or how. But my imagination is initially fueled by the sheer lack of facts noted in the brief genealogy. With a shortage of hard data there is more room for the mind to wander and wonder.

Here is what I know. On January 1, 1858 Andreas is 45 years old and Lena is 47, and they will observe their 26th wedding anniversary on July 7th. Their ages put them near the top for anticipated life expectancy of this era. Lena has already given birth to eleven children, and together the family has grieved the early deaths of four of them. The living children range in age from 4-year-old Samuel to 25-year-old Johannes with a 9-year-old pre-teen, three teen-agers, and a

20 year old in between—all under the same roof. You think you have it rough?

The realities of a large household, a harsh climate with long winters, the workday chores of farm life, and what I assume to be mid-19th century poverty are tempered, however, by some information gleaned from historical texts and land records. Poverty was real, land was scarce, but there was some good news.

"Peace, pox, and potatoes" was the explanation offered by a Swedish bishop to describe what was new in the country. Sweden was not at war, and had not been since wars with Russia and Denmark had ended by 1814. A vaccine for smallpox had been discovered, and infant mortality statistics were diminishing. Potatoes could now supplement bread when no other food was available, so these three factors— "peace, pox, and potatoes"—enhanced the quality of life and extended the life expectancy of Sweden's people. With more peaceable times, healthier people, and more food the population was growing. Isn't that good news? Yes, but there's not enough land. Bad news. Farmers had to produce more food to nourish a growing populace, but the limited land broken into smaller plots couldn't do the job.

What would happen to the children of Andreas and Lena? The parents were old; their days were numbered. When the parents were gone, the land would go to the oldest son—Johannes. What about the other sons? Was there enough land for five sons and their future families? What about the girls? Perhaps the daughters would marry and move, but what if they didn't? What about their children? What about the land? It is in the nature of parents to worry about the future for their offspring.

What could the family do? They were already planning for their future. The children were being taught to read and write. The area churches offered the opportunity to learn, so the children went to school. And the family already lived in a more than adequate home. Historical records note that by 1855 Andreas and Lena owned their own land and had built their own home. They began their married life as a hired hand and a milkmaid, but they worked hard and prospered, and their home bore witness to their labors.

Here is the data: They built their house on the Lund Westergarden farm (part of the previously mentioned Lund By)—five rooms on the first floor and two rooms in the attic with dimensions of 34' by 28' and the highest point of the ceiling at 19'. Their barn had a two-foot-tall rock foundation and measured 60' X 28', including an open area for threshing, storage for hay and small grain, and a stable for cattle and horses. They had their own brewery—a peat covered roof enclosing a building 28' X 20'. Homebrew was a staple of Swedish farm life, and owning your own brewery was a sign of the family's comfortable wealth. The nearby peat bog—their fuel source—required them to build a shed to dry and store their fuel. Other amenities included a pig house, root cellar, two wells, and a garden including a small orchard with apple and cherry trees.

It appears that by January 1, 1858—my arbitrarily chosen date—the family was already putting in place a plan to leave Sweden and come to America. Who knows when the plan originated, but there must have been conversations among the cousins—Andreas Larsson and his younger cousins, the Andreasons—A.P. and Daniel. (Remember: Larsson became Lundborg and Andreason became Broberg in the new land.)

These three young men were raised as neighbors in addition to being cousins. Their families knew one another. By 1829 all three were orphans. Andreas' parents were both gone by the time he turned 13, and there is evidence that his mother's brother became a guardian for him. By 1829 the parents of the young Broberg brothers had both died. A.P. was 10, and Daniel 5, and Andreas was the older, wiser cousin—now 17. Families took care of each other. Uncles and aunts, even older siblings, stepped into parental roles. Family gatherings were a daily occurrence in this closely-knit rural area, and when the cousins were together they did far more than tell stories about their common great-grandfather, Torsten. They dreamed and schemed. Soon they were young adults, then grown men with wives and children, and the dreams were becoming plans. They were planning to go to America. If 1858 was the year for the plan to move into its action phase, there had been 29 years of conversations among these cousins since they had been left without parents.

Why leave when life is good? Good home, big family, friends and neighbors—weren't these enough good reasons to stay where you were? Not all was well, however. Religious life felt stifling to many Swedes. The state-run church had a lot of power over peoples' lives. In order to leave the country Swedish people were required to experience what looks like a kind of "exit-interview" with their parish pastor. In fact, those interviews are now part of the important records that provide us information about our ancestors.

Perhaps there were other complaints about life in their homeland, but the most compelling reason to leave was the excitement of adventure—a new beginning with prospects for an even brighter future for the younger generation. Stories of a life beyond Sweden's borders in the new country of America were thrilling to hear. Good farmland, lots of it, lakes and trees just like home, land enough for all—including our children! These were adventuresome people, not desperate, and they had the means and the reasons for a new experience. Staying home meant the possibility of losing some of what they had already accumulated because the coming land reform act would re-apportion the farmland. Leaving was risky but more hopeful. They were a strong family with personal and financial resources, and they had a plan based on years of dreaming.

Was January 1, 1858 the day for the family meeting? Probably not. But some how at some time important decisions were made. Who knows exactly when, but here are the documented events which occurred that year and soon thereafter, none of which could have happened without a plan.

1. On July 13, 1858, oldest son Johannes, along with brothers Anders and Lars and one of their cousins, arrived at the port in Boston, Massachusetts. They sailed from Gothenburg on the good ship Minona to begin their adventure as the scout team preparing to welcome the rest of the family to Minnesota later. They knew people already living in Minnesota. Relatives and friends of the family were already settled in Carver County west of what would become the Minneapolis/St. Paul area and Ottertail County more to the northwest. Family stories tell of the young Lundborg men stopping in Carver County and being advised to go north. Other stories are told of trapping and trading near the Red River Valley farther to the west in order earn some income for land purchase, but no documentation has been found yet. Minnesota was a brand new state in 1858 filled with opportunities galore, the best place for three strong young brothers ages 26, 21, and 17. In addition, there were now three less mouths to feed at the home place in Sweden, plus more room, but more work.

2. Early in 1859 the oldest daughter, Sarah—now 17—married Johannes Lundquist, and they began their life together on his family's farm. Before her parents could leave Sweden, Sarah gave birth to a baby girl and was already expecting the next child. Perhaps this information doesn't bear witness to the

notion of careful planning, but it is worth noting there is now one less mouth to feed and one less ticket to purchase from the budget of Andreas and Lena. The birth of grandchildren, however, must have tugged at their heartstrings as they pondered the inevitability of saying farewell to a beloved daughter, extended family, and grandchildren.

3. By October 1859 Andreas sold his farm, and the family moved a few miles away to work the Saxtorp farm, which they rented. They have liquidated their assets, lightened their load, and are ready to leave Sweden when the time is right. This plan was made to avoid the penalties of the land reform act that would have diminished the family's property, and it served to position them to leave Sweden when the time was right.

4. In 1861 son Gustaf, now 22 years old, moved to Gothenburg, according to the church records. It's three years after three of his brothers left for America, and a few months before the rest of his family came to Gothenburg to set sail together for their new home. Did he have a job? Was he bored and simply ready to leave home? I'd love to know. These church records, signed by Pastor Floberg, reveal something else unique about Gustaf. He was the only family member who didn't read well. The pastor also notes that all the family members had studied Luther's *Small Catechism*, even memorized it, but not a one of them understood it. Was this a fact or a pastoral judgment call reflecting a dim view of his exiting parishioners? Gustaf did leave home before his parents, sister Johanna, and brother Samuel did, but they all eventually left the country together from Gothenburg, the big port city on Sweden's west coast.

5. In June, 1861, Andreas and Lena (now Lundborg), along with their children Gustaf, Johanna, and Sam-

uel, arrived at the port of Boston, Massachusetts. Within a month they would rendezvous in Minnesota with their older children who left home in 1858.

6. Also in June, 1861, A.P. and Daniel Broberg, along with their wives and children, arrived at Quebec. By July 15 they would be in Minnesota and reunited with Andreas and Lena and all their children, except for Sarah in Sweden.

The decisions were made. The families moved in pursuit of a dream to begin anew and do what was right for the younger generation. Oh, the power of a dream, a vision for a new future, and a desire to better the lives of their children!

Chapter Four

✺

A New Start

D id they write letters? Did anyone keep a diary? If only there were a personal journal providing a record of the trip from the Tåstorp Farm to a plot of land in west central Minnesota! No such luck. Time spent aboard ship from Gothenburg might have measured four to six weeks with a stop perhaps somewhere in England. From the landing spot in North America—Boston for the Lundborgs and Quebec for the Brobergs—at least another month was spent in travel to reach Minnesota. Traveling cross-country was done by a combination of rail, foot, water (Great Lakes and big rivers), and wagon—a journey calling for courage, stamina, and patience. Thousands more would make this same journey in the coming years, but the later travelers would experience a few more creature comforts.

Picture the travelers. There's the Broberg party of two families. The men, A. P. and Daniel are 41 and 37. Their wives are younger. Christina is 35 with four children 15, 12, 9, and 6; Anna Stina, a mere 29, but six months pregnant in addition to having a 6 year old and a 3 year old to watch over.

The Lundborg party consists of the parents now 49 and 50, Gustaf 22, Johanna 12, and 8-year-old Samuel. The cost of following the dream must have seemed very high during these days of travel. The logistics for the three much younger Lundborg brothers who left home in 1858 were nothing compared to the issues faced by families immigrating with children.

But finances were not an issue. Maybe that's an overstatement, but the records indicate the Lundborgs and Brobergs were not poor peasants barely making a living in the old country. It's entirely possible they were coming to America to get rich-er. That sounds crass, especially in these 21st century days when personal wealth is equated with political power that easily leads to corruption. But the image of a politically powerful 19th century Swedish farmer is an oxymoron. Power didn't get them to America. Hard work and careful planning did, and some extra money didn't hurt.

The accumulated Lundborg wealth began when Andreas and Lena married in 1832 and began work at the Tåstorp farm as a hired hand and a milkmaid. They slowly moved up the economic ladder, as did the Brobergs, so they could set aside the money for the journey of their life. But they also saved enough to pool their funds to pay the travel costs for an additional family—the Åmans. Sven Johanson Åman, 42, was a logger and builder born in Algutstorp and known by the Lundborgs and Brobergs. He and his wife and two children, a nine-year-old son and 7-year-old daughter, made the journey later, arriving in August of 1861. Once settled in America as a neighbor and friend to Andreas, Sven and his family could repay the travel costs by felling the trees and building the homes while the Lundborgs and Brobergs broke the land. It was a masterful plan crafted by creative imaginations and shrewd thinking—along with some gold coins. Oral tradition mentions a vest with gold sewn into the lining serving as a personal bank. The Broberg family stories reveal that gold was divided among all family members aboard ship—children included—so the entire fortune wouldn't be lost at once. Children? Clothing? Perhaps both were more easily accessible than a bank.

Swedes had been coming to America since the 1600's when the New Sweden colony was established in the area of New Jersey and Delaware. After 1861 the flood of Swedish immigrants began in earnest. But in 1861 the Lundborgs and Brobergs were part of a trickle of newcomers heading for Minnesota. Minnesota became a state in 1858, and a travel industry with brochures and ads had barely begun. Word of mouth slowly worked its influence from the new land back to the old country. But there already were Swedish settlements in Carver County, west of today's Twin Cities, and Chisago County to the north. Most likely, the Lundborg young men who arrived three years earlier, stopped in Carver County to consult the Swedish residents who had come from Västergötland and settled there. They learned that land to the north was opening up in Monongalia County (now assimilated into Kandiyohi County) where Norwegians had settled, and this land was on the northwest edge of Minnesota's settled land. Dakota Territory was right across the border, and that was a place for Indians, trappers and traders, but not many settlers—yet.

How did they procure land to live on and work? Here's where the tension in the story begins because the very land the Lundborgs "discovered" on or around July 15, 1861, had been lived on, cared for, and enjoyed for several centuries by two major tribes of Indians who had no thought of "owning" the land. The area becoming known as the new state of Minnesota had been the home of the Ojibwe and Dakota, and this area of what was now being called Monongalia County was directly on the edge of the "big woods"—a phrase to name the tribes' prime hunting grounds.

White people, particularly the French, who knew how to work with Ojibwe and Dakota had been trapping, trading, and inter-marrying in order to build social relationships that allowed all to share the bounty of the land from the mid 1600's until the early 1800's. But when expanding the frontier became the desired goal of the United States government, and the issue of "settling" the land became the means, tension arose between the Indians and newcomers. Treaties calling for ceding Indian land in return for money and food were initiated and consummated leaving Indians land-poor and angry and broken treaties scattered on the prairie. Reservations were created for the Indians to live on, and coercive plans to take away the language and culture of the Dakota and Ojibwe nations brought humiliation to this race of people. The 1851 treaty with the Dakota opened what would become the floodgates for settlers hungry for new land.

The Lundborgs and Brobergs settled on land never before owned by anyone. Owning was a European concept, alien to this continent's first residents. But as early as the 1820's the US government began to survey, measure, and give names to parcels of land even in areas that had not achieved territorial or statehood status. These immigrant families heard about the available land, looked it over, deemed it worthy, and transported their few possessions to move on to "their" land. In the history of Arctander Township where this land was located, the Lundborgs are noted under the category of "preemptors and squatters." They claimed their land by moving there and beginning to build a place to live. They began the necessary paperwork to transfer ownership to their names, and in time it would become theirs. Occupying the land and beginning to improve it was the first step on the way to becoming a landowner. A cruel irony in this story is that the Lundborgs' deed for ownership to the land was not issued until 1863, and the named owner was Gustaf Lundborg—one of the sons killed by the Dakotas in 1862.

The 1905 Arctander Township records name the Broberg brothers as "settlers," rather than "preemptors or squatters." Why the difference? The Brobergs purchased two plots, and the paperwork for one was completed by 1862. Did that qualify them for status as "settlers"? I'm not sure. No matter what their legal position in relationship to the land, all four households were now living on it.

Lundborgs and Brobergs alike purchased their land with the help of the Scrip Warrant Act of 1855, which made it possible for them to buy land from a military veteran who had been awarded the deed for service to their country. The Lundborg's land came from Jesus Serano, a veteran of the Mexican War, and the Brobergs purchased their land from Anselmo Garcia, also a veteran of the Mexican War. In addition, the Brobergs bought another piece of land from a navy veteran of the War of 1812. Each plot purchased measured 160 acres, one quarter of a section.

My newcomer relatives took charge of what amounted to 640 acres of land and began living on it as if it were their own. They had the legal right to it in the eyes of the state of Minnesota and the United States Government. At the same time, the Dakota people, who had lived off the land with no concept of land ownership for more than 200 years, saw the land they had enjoyed for ages become no longer accessible to them. Government authorities were telling the Dakota to move onto a 10-mile-wide strip of land along the Minnesota River to the south and to stop hunting and learn how to farm.

Whose land was it? Who had the right to live in a particular place? By whose standard should those questions be considered? Two very differing cultures offered two very different answers, and they both lacked the common language necessary to resolve the issues. Hindsight suggests the governments of the state of Minnesota and the United States both lacked the will to resolve these issues. My reading of history tells me the plan was for the Indians to simply go away. When that didn't happen, the next plan was more sinister. The notion of "first come, first served" was not inclusive of the Indians. It only applied to the white settlers afflicted with land fever.

But another dimension to this part of the story was the division among the Dakota people themselves concerning how to adapt to the struggle for land. All of the Dakota felt the injustice of the fraudulent treaties, but they possessed no unanimous response. Indian chiefs who had traveled east to meet government leaders saw the vast numbers of white people, the populated cities, the soldiers, and the weapons and realized their very survival was in jeopardy. There were those who began to strategize for the sake of survival, choosing to endure the hurt and humiliation, doing whatever was necessary for their people to live. Some have named that strategy as "becoming like the enemy," and if becoming a Christian, cutting the hair, and learning to farm meant the survival of the people, they were willing. But among the young who were rightfully angry, the passion for vengeance dominated their thoughts, and they were ready to kill or be killed. This division within the Dakota nation has been called by some a conflict bigger than that between the Dakota and the white settlers. Dakota culture is very democratic, so even when a group united and asked Little Crow to lead them to war, that decision was not binding to all. The coming war was not the will of all the Dakota people, and innocents on both sides would suffer greatly.

Beginning around mid-July 1861 when the Lundborgs and Brobergs came together to settle their land, they would have a bit more than a year before everything would begin to unravel. What would they accomplish in that year?

They had the natural resources of abundant water in the lakes nearby and a supply of fuel, construction materials, and wild game in the woods. Their greatest resource, however, was the abundant, youthful energy of their families that could accomplish the constant hard work necessary to begin their new life. Many hands contributed to the sawing, building, plowing, hunting, cooking, baking tasks that were necessary for survival. They possessed familiarity with the land and the climate because the area was so similar to the part of Sweden that had been their home. And they knew one another well enough to stick together when the snow piled high and the cruel winds blew through their crude cabins. Which it would do in that first winter of 1861–62.

They felled trees and began to build homes. They broke ground and began to plant seed. They found ways to procure food through the purchase of supplies and by fishing, hunting and trapping game. They became part of a Lutheran Church being created in the area. They made acquaintances with their Norwegian neighbors to the east and the south. They met some of their Indian neighbors who stopped by occasionally and traded furs and meat for milk and bread. They hiked to St. Cloud or Paynesville for supplies. Most important, they were able to survive their first winter. No small feat.

Chapter Five

❧

Tuesday, August 19, 1862

Let's stop time around noon on this day, 24 hours before the normalcy ended and chaos began. The residents of these four households have enjoyed amazing success in their great adventure, and they have reason for being optimistic about their future. They are alive, the first harvest is a good one, and there is new life to celebrate. Daniel and Anna Stina's baby, little Johan Albert (Baby John), who was the first American born member of this extended family last October, is now 10 months old. And 21-year-old Johannes Nilsson, half brother to Christina (Mrs. AP Broberg), has just arrived from Sweden and is living with them. His presence offers more hands for the necessary outdoor work, and he is affectionately known as Uncle John to all the children. The Åman family arrived last August, just a month after the first four families began to settle, and now the Swensons, another family from Västergötland, is living nearby—possibly with Andreas and Lena. And Johannes Lundborg is married. Late last fall he took young Kristina Larson as his bride. And they're expecting! Their baby is due in about a month. The parents, grandparents, uncles, aunts, and cousins are thrilled! There is strength in numbers, and the numbers are increasing.

The early and bountiful wheat harvest warms the hearts of these farmers, and something else makes them hopeful— a celebration. There will be a wedding sometime early in the fall after the first frost, and everyone knew Andreas Lundborg bought some wine and carefully set it aside to be shared at the upcoming wedding. Such a purchase was extravagant, luxurious, and pointed to a great cause for celebration. We will never know who was planning to be married, but we will hear again of the wine.

There is always cause for worry, and they had their reasons. Their new country is at war—with itself. Since February 12, 1861, the armies of the Union and the Confederacy have been at war over the cause of states' rights, and the fundamental states' right that is splitting the country is the issue of slavery. Southern states chose to secede from the Union rather than have a federal government tell them that slavery will not be allowed, and the Northern states chose to fight in order to not allow the secession. Young men from all the states are enlisting to serve their country, and fierce battles claiming many lives are taking place far to the east and south of Minnesota. But Minnesotans know what's happening, and the residents of this newly settled farm country are spending too much time saying farewell to their sons who go off to war. Johannes Lundborg is giving the matter strong consideration, and later he will enlist. But for now, this war is one of their worries.

Did they worry about the Indians? How much did they know? How worried were they? I think our immigrant ancestors were somewhat naïve, so maybe this fits into the category of "issues they should have worried about." They had never lived among people other than Swedes. Their closest neighbors now were Norwegian immigrants, and even though their languages were similar, the bonds between these fellow Scandinavians were not strong. The Swedes saw the Indians and obviously recognized their differences, but did they have any awareness of Indian history and culture? I don't think so. Blessed are the ill-informed, for they shall not worry much. If they had been worried, they might not have settled so close to the big woods, the territory's best hunting grounds.

Also, they were living far enough away from the hub of communication in this new state that they seldom saw a newspaper. If they did, could they read it? How fluent were they in English, the language of their new land?

Their pastor, Rev. Andrew Jackson—a fellow Swede— spoke English, was well read, and traveled around enough to gather word-of-mouth information. He knew about the Dakota Indians who killed five white settlers on Sunday, August 17, a day's horseback ride away—about 40 miles. But maybe he considered it an isolated incident, the reckless behavior of young men who had too much to drink. Many others in the area also knew this information by now, but the Swedish households did not.

It's possible Jackson also knew about incidents at both the Upper Agency (Granite Falls) and Lower Agency (Redwood Falls) of the reservation, both about a day's ride away, on July 14th and August 4th when the Indians demanded their promised food and money and were refused. Government agents relented enough to distribute some food, and outright rebellion was avoided, but the simmering tensions were near the boiling point.

Jackson might not have known about Monday morning, August18[th], when Little Crow led the attack on the Lower Agency killing agents and traders. Later that same day Captain John Marsh and about 25 of his soldiers were killed as they tried to approach the agency to offer help. Hindsight provides us with that knowledge and causes us to feel the terror on the settlers' behalf, but it's entirely possible these families were not concerned at all.

Whatever worries there might have been about the Civil War and a possible Indian war moved to the background on a beautiful late summer day when the air was filled with hope. Tomorrow the pastor will come by for a visit, and he will lead his small Swedish flock in a service of worship. How fitting to have an opportunity, when things are going well, to give thanks to God.

Chapter Six

❧

Introducing The Narrator

Not many family stories make a point of including their pastor in the plot, but there are some good reasons to make an exception. Perhaps the most obvious reason is that I am a pastor, and I have a tendency to notice pastors in whatever stories I encounter. In addition, a pastor played a significant role in my family when I was a child. In the summer of my tenth year, 1954, my father died suddenly, and within an hour the new-to-the-community Lutheran pastor knocked at our door and introduced himself. Within his first year in Milan he buried my father, married my brother, married my sister, buried my brother's first born, and baptized my sister's first born. His relationship with me planted seeds of influence that began to sprout when in my second year of college the notion of becoming a pastor first sounded like a possibility.

My pastor-seeking radar lit up the more I learned about Rev. Andrew Jackson and realized not only the numerous connections with my relatives over the years but also the significant place he occupied in the newly emerging Swedish Lutheran Church in America—specifically, in the Augustana Synod, a group of congregations. Allow me to introduce the

Lundborg's pastor before he becomes the narrator of their story.

He wasn't always known as Andrew Jackson. He was born February 11, 1828 as Andrew Olafson, son of farmer Olaf Jakobson, on the Swedish island of Tjörn, 35 miles north of Gothenburg in the state of Västergötland. Upon entering high school he became Andrew Dahlin. Why? No reasons are cited in the records, but he was known to be a colorful but very capable student. He had eleven siblings so the family farm was crowded, but this bright young man took summer jobs as a live-in tutor, and this brought him to the home of a sea captain who opened Andrew's mind to the wonders of the greater world beyond the waters. In 1852 at age 24 his strong academic accomplishments seemed of little value compared to an opportunity to see the world, and he went to sea as the ship's steward accompanying Captain Klase on a journey to New York. What excitement for this farm-grown landlubber! And in New York he did the unthinkable—he jumped ship, and his story took a dramatic turn.

He and three friends were enticed by a "seamen's runner"—the equivalent of a ship crew's head-hunter—who offered them more pay to do less work on a better ship. But the recruits were required to pay the runner for the privilege of signing on, and that's when they realized they had been duped. Fleeing the runner who wanted his money and Captain Klase who wanted them back at work, the young men sought refuge in a sleazy hotel, and while signing in decided to use fictitious names. That's when Andrew Olafson Dahlin became Andrew Jackson. It was a spur-of-the-moment decision made purposefully to save his neck, and he chose Jackson's name because he had heard of and admired "Old Hickory," the seventh US President, who served from 1829 to 1837. Besides, Jackson was close to Jakobson, Andrew's father's surname, and the letter J might be his mnemonic tool to remember his new name under pressure.

As this New York adventure was concluding, Jackson realized returning to Sweden was no longer a good idea. He sold some clothing and with 75 cents in his pocket began walking out of New York City with a plan of following the railroad tracks to Galesburg, Illinois, where he knew other Swedes had settled. Hungry and fearful he slept in haylofts and worked where he could. His first effort at physical labor was in a brickyard where he tolerated the work far better than he could endure the vermin in the sleeping quarters, so he continued on until he found a job in a sawmill north of New York City, well off the path towards Galesburg. But this job was a good one because he was the only Swede among an Irish crew, and by daily interacting with these English-speaking Irishmen he became fluent in the language of America. He also toughened up by building a working-man's calluses on his hands, and learned to fight well enough to acquire the nickname "Goliath," and stayed on the job for five years.

By 1858 he traveled west and was attached to a community of Swedes in Waupaca, Wisconsin. These Swedes recognized the sounds of education in Jackson's voice, so he became a teacher to the community's children and a guide to groups traveling farther west who needed a translator. That is what brought him to the area in Minnesota where the Lundborgs and Brobergs would settle. He arrived in Monongalia County to stay in the summer of 1859.

He was religious enough to be asked to read sermons from a book to various pastor-less communities on the frontier. Even so, he went through a dramatic conversion experience with the help of some notable Swedish Lutheran pastors, Eric Norelius and Peter Carlson, who both encouraged him to study to become a pastor. Seminary training was brief—ten months in Chicago—and his friends in the community in Minnesota respected him enough to help fund his training by making and selling butter and sending him the cash. He was ordained as a pastor of the newly organized

Augustana Synod on June 9, 1861 in Galesburg, Illinois. Yes, he finally made it to Galesburg. And he was called as the missionary pastor to a congregation in Minnesota, a newly settled area north and west of present day Willmar, MN. A church with no building was organized October 26, 1861, just three months after the Lundborgs and Brobergs moved into that very area, and Pastor Jackson says of his parish: "My field of activity as pastor contained four small congregations, located respectively at Eagle Lake, Nest Lake, Welson Prairie, and Norway Lake. In the last named congregation I had two preaching stations, the one beside Norway Lake for the Norwegians who lived around that lake, and the other preaching station (at West Lake—now Monson Lake) was to accommodate a few Swedish families who had made their homes five to six miles west of Norway Lake." (from an unpublished manuscript in the archives at Gustavus Adolphus College) This was how Jackson became the pastor of the Brobergs and Lundborgs.

Jackson began a confirmation class in the fall of 1861 so that a number of young Swedish men and women who had been without a church and a pastor might prepare to receive the sacrament of holy communion. Among his students were Anna Stina Broberg whose story we will hear later, and a young woman, Miss Kristina Sampson (other sources give her name as Swenson) of Becksville in Meeker County, who would soon become Mrs. Andrew Jackson and the mother of their three children—Hanna, Esther, and Joseph Ansgar (named after St. St. Ansgar, 9th century missionary priest designated the "apostle to the north" who helped bring Christianity to Sweden and namesake for the academy Jackson would later serve in Carver County). They settled near Nest Lake.

It was on a Tuesday, November 26, 1861 that Pastor Jackson stopped at the Lundborg settlement and presided at the marriage of Johannes Lundborg and Kristina Larson. Just prior to that event Johannes had been elected as a deacon of the church. Rev. Jackson, meet the Lundborgs!

Even on the wide-open frontier of a new country, church life had its tensions. I'm sure there were some of these Swedes who had grown weary of the state run church of the old country, and it can't be assumed all were overly eager to embrace the care of a pastor again. State church pastors in Europe possessed a power that many immigrants despised. This new land promised freedom from oppression, and in the minds of some, the Swedish church had wielded an oppressive power. How eager was the 50-year-old, shrewd, strong-willed farmer Andreas Lundborg to welcome this educated 34-year-old fellow Swede to be his pastor?

And it is worthy of note that there were signs that part of Jackson's extended parish was already looking for a new pastor. On July 18, 1862, just more than a month before the Indian war erupted in Monongalia County, some of the Norwegian residents of the Norway Lake area who chose not to affiliate with the Swedes in this congregation, were entertaining a Norwegian pastor—Rev. B. J. Muus—who was visiting in the Engen household, and they invited a few of Jackson's Norwegian members to attend. In his journals Jackson notes that Muus, whose name means "mouse" in English, was "nibbling away at my members, working on them" to leave. Yes, pastors are capable of petty jealousies. (Interesting footnote to this story is that Pastor B.J. Muus went on to become the founder of St. Olaf College in Northfield, MN, and Pastor Jackson was instrumental in founding Gustavus Adolphus College not too far away in St. Peter. Perhaps maturity diminished their pastoral insecurities.) This new country allowed its citizens to choose their church and even their pastor. Should I be surprised to learn even 19th century Lutheran churches in America were divided? Back then language and ethnic background—even cultures like Swedish and Norwegian that seem to be so similar—could easily separate people even as they lived as neighbors in an isolated outpost. Their intertwined histories evidently left room for lots of bad memories. Should I be slow to believe even now when church members leave for greener pastures?

Jackson traveled among his parishioners in a horse drawn wagon and presided at services in the peoples' homes, and it was his pastoral calling that brought him to the farm home of Andreas and Lena Lundborg on August 20, 1862 to lead worship for his parishioners. There wasn't a church building to come to, so he came to them. He couldn't stop at four places on Sundays, so he came to the West Lake people on a Wednesday. And this would be the final service led by Pastor Jackson for this little community. A day filled with late summer beauty, warmed by sunshine on the reverent gathering of friends, would disintegrate into violence, tragedy, and great human loss. With the deaths of thirteen from his congregation and the governor's command to vacate the area, Jackson would become a pastor without a church. On August 20 he would become part of a defining event in the life of my family, and there would come a time when they would meet again in Carver County.

In the summer of 1863 Pastor Jackson relocated to Carver County where he first became a missionary-at-large and the fundraiser for a Swedish school established as an academy named St. Ansgar's. It was begun at Vasa Church near Red Wing by Pastor Norelius, but it was moved to East Union in Carver County where a two story log structure was built to house the school and the students' residence. From 1863–1876 Jackson served as the Director and Principal of the school and pastor of the parish at West Union. As part of his missionary-at-large responsibilities he traveled north again in 1865 to the Nest Lake Congregation and helped them re-organize, admit new members, and eventually call a new pastor in 1867.

From 1876–1890 Jackson continued with the church at West Union and helped with the process that transformed St. Ansgar's from a "school for Swedes" into a church college that took the name of Gustavus Adolphus and moved to St. Peter, Minnesota.

The restless young student from an island off Sweden's west coast who jumped ship and ran from the law, who learned to fight and talk English among the Irish in a saw-mill, and who served as guide/translator/teacher to other Swedish families moving towards Minnesota, was maturing into a devout Christian called to pastoral ministry, and was emerging as a leader in the early days of the Augustana Synod of the Swedish Lutheran Church, and Gustavus Adolphus College.

From 1890–1892 he was the financial solicitor for Gustavus while living in St. Paul. From the winter of 1893 until his death July 23, 1901 he was the pastor of Rush Lake Swedish Evangelical Lutheran Church near present day Stanchfield, MN, fifty miles north of Minneapolis. Here he was particularly honored for his "solid sermons, his straight-forward lovable personality and friendly social manner, and, of course, his sincere piety."

In 1870 Jackson was present to provide pastoral care for Andreas and other family members when my great, great grandmother Lena died. She died at 60 years of age, and even though no medical records will testify to this conclusion, it was at least partially due to a broken heart from grief and shattered dreams. Andreas would outlive her by 21 years. Although the records state she died at West Lake, she was buried at the cemetery of West Union Lutheran Church of Carver County where Jackson was now the pastor. That's a long way to ride in a wagon. Today it's more than two hours in a car, but the highway does not go cross-country. I picture Andreas with his 17-year-old son Samuel leaving West Lake traveling in a horse drawn wagon carrying Lena's coffin to her final resting place. He said farewell to his three sons buried where they fell, and a young daughter newly married and settling in to her home, and I know he's never coming back.

From 1863–1890 Pastor Jackson tended to the families of my great grandparents Johannes and Kristina Lundborg and their 12 children and to my great uncle and aunt Samuel and Anna Lundborg and their six children. Of those 18, 17 were born while Jackson was serving as their pastor. Imagine the births, baptisms, confirmations, high school graduations, and weddings he either attended or presided at for members of my family! I know he also presided at the marriage of my grandparents, August and Anna Lundborg, and both of them were musicians in the West Union Church, assisting Jackson in leading worship. And he was a colleague of my grandmother's half brother, Matthias Wahlstrom, an early president of Gustavus.

As an inexperienced, brand new pastor at 34 years of age, the counsel he offered my family on August 20, 1862 was questionable at best. He withheld information the family should have known, and in a dangerous situation he advised the men to not pick up their guns, counsel they did not appreciate. I don't know if Andreas or Samuel trusted him again after that experience, but in a small, rural community adversaries can't hide from one another. I'm certain they saw one another frequently, and I'm willing to wager the rough edges of their relationships grew smoother over the years.

From 1893–1901 Jackson served one more congregation, the people of Rush Lake Swedish Evangelical Lutheran Church in Chicago County. He died July 23, 1901 and is buried in the cemetery of what is now called Calvary Lutheran Church in Stanchfield, MN.

In 1927 a park was set aside for the purpose of regular gatherings to commemorate the lives of the 13 Brobergs and

Lundborgs who died in 1862. The Monson Lake Memorial Association planned the very first program in 1927, and the speakers were the Minnesota state governor—Theodore Christianson; the local congressional representative—O. J. Kvale; and one other, perhaps lesser known—Joseph Ansgar Jackson, a St. Paul attorney and the son of Rev. and Mrs. Andrew Jackson. Pastor Jackson had died 26 years before this event, and the invitation to his son represented the respect and affection this community had for the Jacksons.

Jackson was known as a good and kind pastor to many, and church historians have affirmed his accomplishments. I think he did his best and cared well for my family, and through my reading of the story of his life I have come to know him well enough to have his voice tell the story of the day when 13 of my relatives lost their lives. I made a pilgrimage to Stanchfield, Minnesota to see his grave in the summer of 2012 where I said then what I say now, "Thank you, Pastor Jackson, for faithfully caring for my family through difficult years."

Chapter Seven

❧

Wednesday, August 20, 1862
(Perhaps this is how Rev. Andrew Jackson
could have told this story in the late summer of 1890,
at the age of 62, eleven years before his death.)

I regret that I didn't get to know those Lundborg boys. Regrets seem to surface more easily these days as I look back on my life. I find it hard to comprehend all that I have experienced in my years in Sweden and in this new land. So much joy. So much sorrow. Within the same lifetime. The joy has been such a gift—pure, undeserved grace granted by the hand of a merciful God who gave me a new calling, a new land, and opportunities for service I never dreamed possible. But the sorrow still breaks my heart. Those Lundborg boys died so young. And the Broberg children and their parents. And such senseless death! How could I ever forget?

As I live now in my last days on this earth I owe it to the generations to come to tell them what I know, what I witnessed of their relatives. I acknowledge my guilt, my remorse, my sense of responsibility in this story. I can't avoid it. It is a merciful God I have served, and it is God's grace I have trusted, but my heart is still heavy whenever I recall that day in August 1862. When my rational mind prevails, I know I, too, was powerless to affect any change in that fateful moment when violence erupted and rage poured out of all too human hearts. But those right thoughts always meet my well-honed conscience, and my heart is burdened again.

It was Wednesday, August 20, a beautiful day, in what became the horrific year of 1862. The wheat harvest was finished in our part of this still new state of Minnesota, just four years old. There was a spirit of expectant joy in our community about an upcoming wedding. Looking back through the confusion that followed I can't even remember who was getting married. That Swedish settlement had a few families with eligible offspring. All those Lundborg men—Anders, Gustaf, Lars. Johannes, their older brother and such a fine young man—he was one of the first deacons in our church—was no longer available because I had presided at his marriage the previous November. I'll not forget that wedding. In fact, I recall the date of Nov. 26, 1861, so easily because it was the very first wedding I presided at in this Norway Lake Parish. And it was even more memorable given the circumstances of Johannes' age—29—and the age of Kristina, his child bride, just 17. Johann Nilsson (Uncle John they called him), Christina Broberg's half brother, had just come from Sweden, and he was old enough to be eligible. And I think there were some daughters in that family of newcomers, the Swenson's, who had been there for only a month. And I'll not forget Anna Stina Broberg, just 16, barely eligible for marriage, but destined to become a heroic survivor. Could she have been the future bride? I wish I could remember. Strange, isn't it, that the ensuing darkness has swallowed all the joy of that August 20th morning? The plentiful harvest, the prospect of a wedding, plus the celebration of so many new beginnings had filled the settlement with abundant hope. All had survived the arduous journey from the old country, and new opportunities emerged daily. There was land, good land. There was a supportive community of other Swedes with a common language, a common faith, and this new experience was the fulfillment of years of dreaming and hoping. It was all coming true.

Not that it was easy. We were miles from civilization. Our homes were humble at best. And this new country we were adopting, despite its many freedoms, was at war with itself. A great civil war was taking place hundreds of miles away from us, but we felt it. We heard the stories of other immigrant men volunteering to fight in this war. In fact, Johannes Lundborg was preparing to enlist in the Union's cause. There were rumors of conscription, a program to forcibly draft all young men to go to war and a source of great worry for us all. But these burdens were far from heavy on a sunny August day. In fact, we heard that old man Lundborg had purchased a supply of wine he had now hidden away in anticipation of that upcoming wedding, and we looked forward to that celebration soon after the first frost.

It was a work day for me, if you call presiding at a service of worship work. My calling as pastor to these four settlements including the West Lake folks was never burdensome to me. I was filled with thankfulness for the opportunity to use my gifts for the good of my fellow immigrants. I was still in the process of making some kind of a schedule for my visits to each of these communities, and since this West Lake group was scattered onto the far western edge of my larger parish, I seldom could be with them on a Sabbath day. I hitched my horse and buggy that Wednesday morning to travel from my home at Nest Lake and arrived in the later part of the morning hoping to get everyone together for a forenoon service. The Lundborg cabin where Andreas and Lena lived was most centrally located, and I knew the Brobergs, Omans, and Swensons would be there. We could meet outside, and I would preach the gospel to these hard working folks, and we could sing some of the songs they knew from the old days back in the homeland. What a joy for me to bring the good news to these people in my congregation!

They came in their work clothes. In the old country we all might have looked more presentable. There would have been more time for cleaning up, and they would have been dressed in apparel more suited for attending the worship of God. But here we did what was necessary, and all seemed thrilled for the respite from daily chores and the visit from their pastor. I brought with me memories of their past—language and tradition—along with words of hope from their faith. Perhaps that was part of who I was to them—a link to the past tradition and a reminder of the hope often obscured by our hard life. We greeted one another as friends, as children of

God, and we came together in a prayerful spirit. There were stools and crude chairs outside the cabin for all as we gathered in the great sanctuary of nature among a few trees overlooking the rolling prairie, and I stood to begin the service. We had no books, except for my Bible and Psalmbook, so I read and prayed. We sang together, and I preached to them the good news of Jesus. All was fine until I concluded the sermon, fully anticipating more prayers and an appropriate benediction, when we were surprised by a visitor, one of our own, young Peter Broberg—just 7 years old, I think—who walked into our midst with a troubled look on his face. The youngest children often didn't attend the worship with their parents, so they had been together at the Broberg cabins about two miles away. Uncle John was with them, so the parents weren't worried.

I was surprised young Peter had the courage to interrupt us, but I saw that he was upset and understood why his parents stopped the service. He told us the Indians were at the Broberg cabins. They weren't strangers to us because they would stop to beg from us on their journeys to and from their hunting trips to the big woods. In our early days here they frightened us. I knew they could be violent; in fact after one incident I wrote the governor asking him to restrain these warriors in some way. The men were barely clothed in the summer and had no beards. On some occasions they painted their bodies, wore feathers in their hair, and decorated themselves with trinkets. They spoke no English or Swedish, and we didn't speak their language, so I must admit we never understood each other, and we felt hints of a primitive, fearful quality in their presence. Perhaps it was simply their strangeness, their otherness that frightened us. Their voices, even their language, sounded harsh. They seemed demanding when they asked for food. We would never have troubled them in that manner. The most outspoken among us wondered if they were even human, but I always tried to see them as God's children.

The news of their presence at the other cabin was not so troubling, but young Peter said these Indians were acting strange. He was vague in describing what they were doing, but then we saw the fear in his eyes. In an instant the worship was done. The parents of the young children were becoming alarmed, and there was a flurry of activity. The ensuing events blur together in my memory. The power of fear, even in recalling this, is amazing in its capacity to overwhelm the senses.

A. P. Broberg, Peter's uncle, was ready to go right now because the children were in his cabin, but he knew going alone was not wise. Johannes was the first to take action. Mindful of his very pregnant wife, Kristina, and little sister, Johanna, he called to them to walk towards his cabin. He told them he must leave to warn the neighbors, but he wanted them to stay together, and then he left to find a horse to seek help and spread the warning. None of these families had horses. They worked with oxen in the field, and now they needed a beast capable of moving in a hurry. I couldn't spare my horse since I too would be leaving soon but in a different direction to meet my next congregation for their weekly service. We were all too stunned to be thinking clearly, and even now as I recall these events, I question some of our choices.

Old man Lundborg, Andreas, knew what he had to do, and I wasn't surprised. He's always been quick to act and was never one to turn away from trouble. I'm a man of peace, although that had not always been true for me. I had my fill of fighting in earlier years, but I fought with my fists. I knew that guns would quickly escalate any disagreement, and Andreas went into his cabin to get his rifle. Then his boys did the same. Anders, Gustaf, and Lars—25, 23, and 22—were old enough, but even young Samuel had a gun. Nine years old, and he's already carrying a rifle! Living on the frontier called forth a peculiar kind of courage. We needed the guns to hunt, but we also needed protection from the thieves that traveled the trade routes. And we had our guns in Sweden too. The Indians often carried their rifles when we saw them in their hunting parties, so Andreas told the boys to get their guns. "We have to protect ourselves." That's what Andreas said. I thought he was wrong, and I asked them all to leave their guns at home. Don't lead with force, I counseled them. Your guns will provoke them. The boys reluctantly listened to me and laid down their weapons, but old man Lundborg was not persuaded. He trusted his rifle far more than his pastor.

Was I wrong? I told them not to take their weapons, yet I knew full well the possibility of danger. I confess I felt a shiver up my back when I heard what Peter said. I knew far more than I was willing to say. I knew of recent killings done by the Indians—violence we should have expected had we been willing to pay attention to what was happening at the reservation. On the previous Sunday, just three days earlier, a small band of braves stopped at a home in Meeker County, not far from us, engaged their hosts in conversation, invited them to some competitive shooting, and suddenly killed five of them. That took place maybe 35 miles away. I was shocked when I heard it, but many of us thought it to be a solitary event, the action of some drunken young men. I learned this information from some settlers farther east, and I made a conscious decision to not say anything to my church members. I didn't want anyone to be unnecessarily alarmed. I couldn't imagine the Indians actually coming this far to harm any of us. I was blinded by my ignorance. But when I realized how determined Andreas was to take his rifle to the Broberg cabins, my real fears surfaced, and I had to tell him. I had to warn him about what might happen. But I told him not to tell the women. It would not have done them any good to get all worked up, fear-driven and out of control. He gave me a defiant look, began to walk towards the Broberg cabins, and things were never the same between the two of us after that day. His boys were already at a slow trot down the trail following A. P. Broberg, young Peter's uncle. Behind them came armed Andreas with his rifle in hand, along with Sven Åman, both plodding away at their own purposeful gait, able to only wonder what awaited them. We all did what we had to do.

The Lundborgs were all going in different directions while Daniel brought the wagon around to collect the women—his wife Anna Stina, A.P.'s wife Christina, and Andreas' wife Lena—and the children who didn't want to walk. They would travel home by the same route they rode to the Lundborgs. The chaos and confusion governed by fear had us all in motion. Daniel was trying to calm the women, for they were now anxious about the boys back at the cabin—13-year-old Johannes, 10-year-old Andreas, and 4-year-old Alfred. They were under the watchful eye of Uncle John, a young man but old enough to be responsible, but Peter's warning had alarmed the mothers and they had to go see for themselves that all was well. Daniel was in charge of the wagon with the three women, a baby (10 months old John), two children (7-year-olds Peter and Christina), and a teen-ager (16-year-old Anna Stina). This wagonload was not armed at all, and, although capable of more speed than those walking, they began their journey later and arrived at the cabin shortly after the walkers.

I can't tell you all that happened—all that was told to me—but I know you will understand. Such violence as few can imagine was about to take place, and I'm still so grieved to recall what I learned. But what causes me still deeper pain is that I left. I didn't accompany them into what I knew could be a dangerous encounter. Each of us was doing what we thought we had to do, acting out our role in life's great drama—parents went to warn their neighbors and save their children, and the pastor went to his next congregation. I left with no idea what would happen to these dear souls, only praying and hoping for the best. Later that night after I had again preached the good news to another gathering of the faithful, this time at Norway Lake, my last assignment for the day, my heart broke when I heard the news. The worst thing imaginable had happened. Dear God, could I have altered what took place? I did what I had to do, but even now I grieve. But my pain is nothing alongside the grief of the survivors.

A.P. Broberg, father of four of the young children in this settlement, arrived first at his cabin, and the Lundborg boys were there several minutes later. They saw five or six Indians, although more were nearby, and recognized several. Although some were carrying rifles, they were not threatening in any way, it was reported. A.P. and young Samuel joined Uncle John in the cabin to relieve him of his childcare responsibilities, and the children left to wait outside with the Lundborg young men. There was normal conversation between A. P. seated at the table and several of the Indians standing around when at some kind of a pre-arranged signal the Indians took up their rifles and began to shoot. A.P. was killed instantly where he sat, and young Uncle John—newly arrived a month ago from Sweden—now lay dead on the floor. Samuel Lundborg, the 9 year old, went down instantly, with a bullet in the side. In seconds all three in the cabin had been shot, and even though all appeared to be dead, we would learn later that Samuel had been seriously wounded and had played dead in an effort to survive. His acting was so effective that even after he was shot and one of the Indians struck him with the butt of the rifle and searched his pockets assuming he was dead, found nothing and left him.

Quickly the Indians were outside and chasing the children. Several laid down their rifles to pursue the children with their tomahawks, not guns. Perhaps they were saving bullets; who knows? They were child-killers! Did the children know their young lives were about to end? Three boys—13-year-old Johannes, 10-year-old Andreas, 4-year-old Alfred—Broberg brothers and cousins, so young, so tender, were now filled with fear at the sight of these strange adults who were violating the laws of trust between the generations by killing children. I cannot write, even now, what we all heard later about the mutilation perpetrated on these children's bodies, and I wonder if the grace of God can ever extend to those who were capable of such merciless actions.

All of this happened in minutes. Conversation in the cabin so quickly turned into murderous acts, hideous deeds, done to A. P. Broberg, Johan Nilsson, Samuel Lundborg, and the Broberg children. They were all dead—except for Samuel—and soon Anders and Gustaf Lundborg were shot before they could flee. Lars was able to run through a clearing before he was shot in the back of the head, but he kept running, straining to jump the fence when he was shot again. One of the Indians then took a knife to Lars' throat, and his innocent blood was spilled on this new land of ours.

50 yards away old man Lundborg watched the killing of his sons. He and Sven Åman, showing their age, walked more slowly than the boys, so they arrived too late to become victims themselves but early enough to witness these horrendous deeds. Can you imagine the grief of a father watching the murder of his sons? Maybe he cried out because the killers then saw him and Sven and were about to pursue them when the Broberg wagon drew near from the other direction. Here was easier prey. One unarmed man with women and children in a wagon was far more vulnerable than a couple of tough old men carrying at least one rifle. What happened next sounds like the Bible's story of the "Slaughter of the Innocents." The killing of these gentle souls—parents and children alike—could not have been more cruel. One by one the Dakota men mercilessly murdered them. Daniel was shot first while still in the wagon, but the women and children began to run. These young mothers did all they could to spare their children, clinging to the little ones, urging the older ones to run for their lives. The bodies of these lifeless mothers soon lay on the road with little 7 year old Christina and baby John—just 10 months old—beside them. Tomahawks and rifles were the weapons of choice to kill these helpless victims. The two young pioneer mothers fought their attackers, but they had no chance. Having witnessed the murder of their children before they were killed, would they have wished to survive?

Lena miraculously escaped. Cousins 7-year-old Peter and 16-year-old Anna Stina outran their pursuers, hid in the brush, and were later discovered by other members of their settlement, but the massacre was now complete. Mother Christina and her daughter Christina along with Mother Anna Stina and her baby John lay dead at the side of the road. Daniel's body was left in the wagon. In one of the Broberg cabins were the bodies of Uncle John, A.P. Broberg, and Samuel Lundborg. And scattered in the field outside the cabin were the bodies of Anders, Gustaf, and Lars Lundborg, along with the dead children Johannes, Andreas, and Alfred Broberg. Ten Brobergs, almost two entire families of parents and children, were dead. Three Lundborg young men, in the prime of their young adulthood, lay in their own blood. 14 bodies. 13 dead. This great tragedy unfolded in a matter of minutes, but its impact was felt for a lifetime among those who survived. The survivors—these beloved children of God and lambs of my flock—were scattered to the winds to escape their fearsome enemies and they were forever transformed by the events of perhaps 30 fear-filled minutes on a Wednesday afternoon, August 20, in 1862. The months that followed heaped fear upon fear into their scarred surviving souls.

Most of my story has now been told. I wanted to tell you that three of your Lundborg and ten Broberg relatives died such unnecessary and violent deaths, and their story was a solitary incident among a host of stories that were created at a time and in a place where human beings representing two very different ways of being clashed in a struggle to possess land and preserve identity. Some of my contemporaries called the Dakota people "savages." Indeed, their actions toward us were savage. When my heart was broken by the deaths of these people I loved, I was tempted to blame and hate the entire Indian race. In fact, that is what our young state chose to do. We repaid injustice with injustice, taking back their land, hanging many, and eventually expelling this entire tribe. We extracted our vengeance. But time has done some healing work, and I've become aware that our innocent-appearing actions were hostile and threatening to these Dakota people whose land we were usurping. Our nation did not fulfill its promises of money and food. We forced change upon them. We tried to take away their language and their way of living. My Lutheran understanding of God's work in the world causes me to claim my portion of the blame in this sad story. May God forgive us all and grant us new beginnings.

This chapter in the life of the surviving Lundborgs and Brobergs also includes tales of heroism and reunion that I won't tell in detail, but I want you to know this:

—The Indians continued their murderous ways by scattering into the countryside to the east and south. Seven more from our Norway Lake Parish were killed. And they also began to plunder

and loot. Some hard earned and saved gold is now in their hands. They stole food and clothing and some of our treasured trinkets and family remembrances. They stole our livestock and their food. They destroyed our homes, humble as they were. They were accomplishing their mission of spreading fear all across these small settlements, and when we heard the stories later about their attacks at New Ulm, Fort Ridgely, and Wood Lake we wondered if they would prevail in driving us all out of their land. I know our Lord told us to "fear not," but how could we regain courage in the presence of these people who only wanted our deaths?

We learned later that many Indians on that same reservation were completely opposed to this senseless killing. In fact, the Dakota people who did not want war had to stand up to the ruthless warriors, and they helped many settlers to escape. Many white people had been cruel and merciless to their Indian neighbors, and they received severe justice at the hands of some of the Dakota people. But the suffering of the innocents on both sides of this conflict is a dark chapter in human history

—When I concluded the service at West Lake I went east to the home of Thomas Osmundson near Norway Lake to preside at the next worship service of the day. As we were concluding the service there, Johannes Lundborg arrived on horseback with the news of the West Lake killings. We were stunned, almost into a complete lack of response. Finally, we came to our senses, and I realized I must go on to Nest Lake to tend to my wife and warn my neighbors. Early the next morning after spending the night together at the Adams place at George Lake, we all set out for Forest City where we hoped to find safety. I understand all who had been together at Osmundson's retreated to safety at an island on Norway Lake we came to call the "Isle of Refuge." There they could almost walk out to a hidden sanctuary, or float on a log raft in order to be safe from the attackers.

I traveled much during the next days, first going to St. Cloud to find a safe place, then back to the West Lake Settlement to salvage whatever we could find, and back to St. Cloud. With the help of a group of young men with horses our trip back to West Lake was suc-

cessful. We discovered and returned about a hundred head of cattle, some horses, and as much household goods as we could haul. The security of St. Cloud was a welcome sight.

—Lena Lundborg walked east after she fled from the wagon. She heard soon enough what happened, and she saw much of it, and her heart was broken. She stopped at the Glesne's home near Norway Lake, found no one there, and camped out in the rain, then walked north to Lars Olson's in the Lake Prairie Settlement, and with others went on to Paynesville. I can't emphasize enough the power of the dark shadow of fear felt by all the settlers. We were so isolated, so we looked for the safety of a crowd in a more populated settlement. We were anxious to hear news about our loved ones, but we were always fearful of the worst. Lena felt the terror, and saw some of the violence, and she joined the search for a safe place.

—Johannes Lundborg, along with his wife Kristina and sister Johanna also walked east and were providentially reunited with Anna Stina Broberg as she was running away from the killing of her family. Johannes left these three young women hidden in the rushes of a slough between his father's place and Ole Knutson's while he searched for the others. Imagine these frightened young girls huddling together on a stormy, fear-filled night. Kristina, the eldest, was 17 and eight months pregnant. Anna Stina was 16, and Johanna just 13. Johannes eventually made it to the Isle of Refuge by evening after warning others, and then in the post midnight darkness he led a search party that rescued the young women from their hiding place and they all went back to the Isle of Refuge.

—Andreas Lundborg and Sven Åman escaped several harrowing encounters with the Indians, and some have told great stories about this old man who intimidated his younger enemies with courage. With powder too wet to fire, his gun was useless, so he charged the Indians, bravely shouting and cursing, and they fled, waving their blankets to fend off his unseen powers. Eventually, Sven returned to his cabin and his wife and two children, and they were found by Peter Broberg who had escaped from the wagon where his

62

family members were killed. The Åmans and Peter went to the Isle of Refuge where they found safety.

Andreas, upon returning to his cabin alone, found neighbor Ole Swenson, who had been separated from his family. Andreas and Ole hoped to go towards Norway Lake, but they were chased back by Indians. This became another occasion for the courageous, sly old man Lundborg to outwit his pursuers, and they proceeded to the cabin of Ole Knutson at Norway Lake. Johannes had already been there to warn them, so when Andreas and Swenson learned that, they too went to the Isle of Refuge.

The reunions were almost complete. Most everyone was together in the encampment at the Isle of Refuge in Norway Lake except for Lena, and for several more days no one knew where she was. After Wednesday's killings and the night storm, Thursday was a day of confusion as they wondered what to do. On Friday morning, August 22, Andreas Lundborg gathered everyone together, and he was in charge. Their fear had not diminished, but this grieving father led a burial party of ten men with two teams towards the Broberg cabins to do the right thing. They couldn't allow the bodies of their loved ones to remain uncovered. They stopped first at the Lundborg cabins and saw the destruction and were surprised to find blood. That's when they saw Samuel. He was alive! Everyone thought he had been killed, but he played dead and fooled the Indians. He was not well. He had a gunshot wound in his side and had been beaten on his head with a rifle. But he managed to walk and crawl from the Broberg cabin back home and was lying there when he was discovered. What joy in the midst of heartbreak!

Any bit of good news was necessary to fortify the group for the ghastly task of bringing the bodies of their loved ones together for burial. They closed their eyes to the cruel indignities the braves had forced upon their friends and family. Death itself can evoke great pain, but when that death is violent, and the violence is intensified with unnecessary and cruel deeds done to the body—what more can I say? I mention all of this so you can appreciate the loving deed done by these ten men, led by Andreas, in gathering the bodies, cover-

ing them with blankets or whatever could be found, and then gently placing their bodies together in the ground. I'm certain someone in the group uttered those sacred words about "earth to earth, ashes to ashes, and dust to dust." And I know all was done in the "sure and certain hope of the resurrection to eternal life through our Lord Jesus Christ"—words I could have spoken had I been there. That promise was all we could cling to.

They told me that Andreas, whose fatherly grief must have been heart-rending, then showed such kindness to his friends. He found the wine he had set aside for the upcoming wedding, and when all the work was done and they were preparing to move on towards whatever safe haven they could find, he opened the bottles and poured a drink for each one of those workers. I've told you that Andreas could be an intimidating presence, and I know he wasn't a very pious man, and I'm sure he didn't care for me. But what he did with the wine sounds sacramental to me. Pouring a glass to thank his friends must have reminded some of those good folks of the bread and wine shared thankfully in holy communion. Whether he was aware of the overtone of his actions, I do not know. But hearing the story of this generous act touched me. In the midst of such death and darkness a shared cup of wine was a reminder of other blood shed, poured out centuries ago pointing beyond itself to some hope, some light. And if ever there were people in need of hope and light. . . . They found Lena in Paynesville, and what remained of the Lundborg family was now intact. Of the Brobergs only Anna Stina and Peter remained, and they stayed with the Lundborgs as long as they could.

The West Lake Settlement had been wiped out. The little congregation was no more. My parish was scattered, broken. My work was finished. We were ordered to leave. This part of Minnesota was closed down for three years, and few of its original settlers returned. The Lundborgs found safety in St. Cloud for a while, and then in St. Paul. Johannes and Kristina were in Afton when baby Andrew was born September 20. When the time was right they all found their way to West Union in Carver County where they could mourn their losses, nurse their wounds, and try to begin their dream anew.

Later I also came to Carver County working among the Swedes in East Union, raising funds for a school, and helping out however I could. Once again I would be with the survivors of that fateful day as their pastor. Looking back is a painful exercise. Remembering and telling you hurts even now, but maybe it serves to eventually bring healing. That day was so tragic, and we will never forget it. But my witness to you is to tell you I am so thankful to have known these good people, to have served as their pastor, and I'll never forget them. May they rest in peace.

Chapter Eight

℘

AFTER . . .

The county was vacated because there were no means available to protect the residents. Isolated families living in rural areas desperately sought shelter in more populated sections of the state. This attack was the first of many assaults on innocent civilians in the state of Minnesota as Little Crow led some of the Dakota people in a war to drive out all the white people. But the Monson Lake Massacre was unique in that it was the northern most point in the state where settlers were specifically targeted. Many more civilians were killed along the Minnesota River farther to the southwest.

The state was paralyzed by fear as stories of the brutal attacks were publicized. But whatever military resources the state possessed were committed to the Union Army in the early stages of the Civil War. Able-bodied young men were already far away from home enlisted in a struggle that would last three more years. The governor appealed to the President for military help, and local citizens began to form their own militias, and slowly the skirmishes became a war that would be over in six weeks. But those weeks felt like eternity for all who were caught up in the terror.

The Victims

The victims were buried August 22, 1862 at the site of one of the Broberg cabins where they were killed, and they remained there for 29 years. During those years the land's ownership changed, and a family named Monson purchased it and requested government action to move the bodies. In 1891 Minnesota's governor appointed a commission to erect a monument to honor the lives of these settlers in the cemetery of Nest Lake Lutheran Church. Five years later the church's name was changed to Lebanon Lutheran Church. Family members—Johannes, now known as John Lundborg (brother to the Lundborg young men), John Peterson (husband of survivor Anna Stina Broberg), and Erick Paulson (husband of Johanna, sister to the Lundborgs)—faithfully represented their families in arranging for the monument. The victims' remains were removed from the West Lake area on June 19, 1891, to rest in the cemetery of what is now named Peace Lutheran Church in New London, MN.

The site of their deaths was purchased in 1927 by the Monson Lake Memorial Association and became a Minnesota State Park in 1938. Commemorative events held at the park have helped the community remember these victims and this dark moment in Minnesota's history.

Refugee Family

It's a sad sight we have viewed in movies, on the evening news—refugees fleeing for their lives in search of safety. This time we see them in our mind's eye, and they are my relatives. It's a group of settlers looking for a safe place, and we see among them grieving parents Andreas and Lena, Johannes and youthful but very pregnant Kristina, plus four children, including one wounded and one not well. They are homeless, wearing their possessions, traveling light, hopefully in a wagon but maybe on foot. The Lundborg sons and brothers are dead, their homes plundered, two additional children—

now orphans, and one of them seriously ill—are clinging to them. They have been ordered to leave the county because it is too dangerous for survival, and there is no protection for them. The home grown military is far away fighting the Confederacy, and the young state's law enforcement personnel are minimal. An entire state has been terrorized by the brutal attacks that have already killed hundreds of innocent civilians, and the Lundborgs have joined the ranks of what have been called displaced persons, evacuees, refugees, part of the collateral damage of every war. Total civilian casualties would eventually add to more than 500, the largest number of civilian casualties in any state caught up in war with the Indians over land.

And this was a war. For the Dakota warriors this was a war to defend their way of life, their very survival as a people. Were our ancestors the protagonists? Did they seek the destruction of the Indians? Were they part of a master plan to steal the Indian's land? It's impossible to imagine these Swedish immigrants involved in a plot to forcibly remove the Dakota. But it is possible to imagine how many Dakota viewed these settlers as the enemy. The Dakota had already ceded to the US government for little or nothing land they enjoyed for centuries, and the food and money promised as compensation was not there when they needed it. Their simmering anger led to an outburst of violence, and my family was one of many caught in the middle. Remember, the Lundborgs and Brobergs settled on land near to the "big woods," known as the best hunting land in the area. They were white, in the wrong place, at the wrong time. Fight or flight? It was too late. They had to flee for refuge. As if mourning the deaths of 13 loved ones isn't enough, this band of survivors was forced to grieve on the run— traveling light with heavy hearts.

A Baby Born

Are any among them fluent in English? Probably not, so they looked for Swedish help. Andreas and Lena were entrusted with the care of their wounded son Samuel who is 9 and a half years old, 13-year-old daughter Johanna, plus cousins 16-year-old Anna Stina and 7-year-old Peter Broberg. Johannes and Kristina were most likely traveling with their parents in order to assist them, but their situation is even more urgent because Kristina is now more than eight months pregnant. But they certainly weren't alone. Many others abandoning Monongalia and Kandiyohi counties were going east to Paynesville (25 miles), then north to St. Cloud (30 miles), but this group of eight continued on to the St. Paul area (85 miles south). Baby boy Andrew was born September 20, 1862 in Afton, MN, a small community 25 miles east of St. Paul. This was but a stop along the way, and after Afton, when Kristina and her baby boy, named Andrew, recovered enough to travel, Carver County was just 40 miles away, a destination housing enough Swedish friends to promise these weary sojourners a safe rest.

Settling in Carver County was made easier for this couple and their newborn because friends and relatives from the home area in Sweden were already living there. This was the refuge they sought.

Caring for Peter and Anna Stina

Andreas and Lena slowed their journey to take care of young Peter, who suffered terribly. Not yet eight years old and orphaned, he would cling to his cousin Anna Stina for comfort. But when it was learned Peter had typhoid fever, they all came to a stop in Anoka. Winter travel and a serious illness were more than they could handle. Peter and the Lundborgs stayed in St. Paul until after Christmas when he was well enough so he and Anna Stina could go to Carver on their own. There he stayed at the home of John Ahlin for almost a year, and then came under the care of his guardian, Lars Skoog. In 1864 when Anna Stina married, Peter had a new family. When he turned 14 in 1868, Peter moved in with a family friend, Louis Larson, and began attending school in New London where he would make his permanent home. The Swedish version of community services provided lasting, loving care for this young survivor.

Anna Stina also came under the care of a guardian in April 1863, a Mr. Ole Nelson, and in 1864 she married John Peterson, another survivor of the Indian attacks, and they returned to the Nest Lake area where they farmed. She and her husband later moved north to St. Hilaire, another Swedish settlement, located in northwestern Minnesota and farmed there.

A present day descendant of Anna Stina's, speaking at a 2012 gathering for the descendants of the survivors, said Anna Stina's repeated message to all in her family was, "Without the Lundborgs we never would have made it." She lived not only to tell her story but also to tell it gratefully and record it for posterity.

In Sweden

When was this tragic story first told to the relatives in Sweden? This is pure guesswork, and the best guess is the time between these deaths and the day when family, friends, and neighbors in Sweden learned of it must have been several months, perhaps late October before a letter arrived. Telegraph existed, and newspapers carried stories, but for news to move from rural Minnesota to rural Sweden with accuracy, I can only imagine a letter would suffice. A letter had to cross half this continent and most all of the Atlantic Ocean in order to arrive in Sweden. But there is a story of one who had an earlier premonition—Bengt Andreasson.

In our family's first visit to Sweden in 1991 we were lost, unable to find the Algutstorp Church that was our landmark for knowing we arrived where our ancestors had lived. Only when we told the story of "Indians, Lundborgs, and Brobergs" did we receive knowing glances and welcoming smiles and good directions. In 2010 when my wife and I again came to Sweden, we attended a church service at Södra Härene where I knew my great, great grandfather was baptized in 1812. When the members of the local historical group learned we were Lundborgs, they excitedly ushered us to the cemetery and brought us to the grave of Lars Peter Bengtsson. His grave is located close to the church and is very visible even to visitors. Lars Peter Bengtsson is a son of Bengt and Johanna Andreasson. We thought it strange to be taken unexpectedly to the cemetery, but the Bengtsson grave had a story to tell. The story told concerns Lars Peter's father, Bengt Andreasson, who on the day of August 20, 1862, the day when the 13 members of the Lundborg and Broberg families were attacked and killed in Minnesota, Bengt had a powerful experience. Could it have been a dream? A vision? He heard the voices of A.P. and Daniel Broberg cry out to him, "Come and save us! We are in great danger!"

Bengt was their brother-in-law, married to their sister Johanna. Bengt and Johanna were much older than the younger Broberg brothers. Bengt and Johanna were born in 1808 and 1806 respectively, while A. P. was born in 1819 and Daniel in 1824. Bengt and Johanna had responsibility to raise the younger siblings thrust upon them when mother Catrina and her husband Andreas were both dead by 1829 and the boys were so young. Bengt and Johanna saw these boys emerge from childhood, become men, marry and begin their own families before leaving Sweden in pursuit of their dream. Johanna, A.P., and Daniel were siblings, but when Johanna and Bengt married, the brothers looked to this couple as parents. The bonds of family were strong in this relationship.

The oral tradition says Bengt's experience took place at exactly the same time as the deaths of the Brobergs and Lundborgs, and that would have been near 1:00 p.m. in Minnesota and 8:00 p.m. in Sweden on August 20th. So perhaps Bengt's experience was not a dream. 8:00 p.m. seems early for a Swedish farmer to be asleep on a night in August. How shall it be named? A vision perhaps? Even if we don't know how to name it, and if the experience was not simultaneous to the attack, the power of the story can't be diminished— especially for Bengt. Others can choose to deny the validity of a personal story sounding too strange to be true. But Bengt would never forget it. To know that even this much of the story survives to this day bears witness to its power.

How did the experience affect him? Did he tell it all to his family immediately? How did his family and community regard Bengt after hearing him tell this story? One doesn't normally hear of mystical, paranormal spiritual experiences in the context of Swedish Lutheranism, but sensitive souls exist in every context. I have learned to never quarrel with another's religious experience, and perhaps that is how Bengt's community treated him. When the letter arrived informing the family of the massacre, what was it like for Bengt? How did the community regard him then? It would have been easy for him to become the village naysayer, the dissuader who addressed his neighbor's desires to leave their homeland for American prosperity. He didn't want to hear their cries for help also.

Whatever Bengt's experience within his soul and in the constellation of his relationships, the fact that his story not only exists but is on the tip of the tongue of local historians in and around Vågårda today is a tribute to its power. And Bengt's story is a story within a story, for the story of the massacre itself must have served to keep a number of local residents safely remaining in Sweden.

Death Comes to the Survivors

Andreas and Lena Lundborg

Records indicate Andreas and Lena stayed in St. Paul for a year before they went on to Carver County. In 1865 daughter Johanna was confirmed at the church in West Union, and the decree to be away from Monongalia County for three years ended. After this milestone date the family moved back north close to their original settlement. First they came to the Nest Lake area, and in the spring of 1866 they returned to the land at West Lake and farmed a large acreage. Andreas and Johannes filed the paperwork to be compensated for the losses they experienced in 1862. The US Government made available money that was supposed to go to the Dakota people as part of their treaty rights and instead now chose to give it to those who suffered great loss during the 1862 war. At some time the Lundborgs were awarded almost $1500 altogether. Having lost everything plus their three family members, no financial amount could have relieved their suffering. Perhaps there was some small satisfaction in being able to return to the land.

Lena, however, became sick and died suddenly October 18, 1870, at the age of 60. Surprisingly, she was buried in the West Union Cemetery in Carver County even though they had been living in the West Lake area at the time of her death. Maybe this is when Andreas decided the West Lake area was filled with too many sad memories and he was ready to make his home in Carver County. He and Samuel moved south to stay, leaving Johanna behind as the only Lundborg—now Paulson—in Kandiyohi County.

By the time of the 1875 census Samuel, now 22, was married to Anna Maria Johnson, and Andreas was living with the young couple on Samuel's farm in Carver County. Andreas continued to live with Samuel, Anna and their children in Carver County, and perhaps he returned to his former work of being a "hired hand," the work he began back at Tås-torp Farm many years ago, but now he could work for his son. A few days short of his 79th birthday the old man died on January 8, 1891. Andreas was buried beside Lena in the West Union cemetery. Their story was hardly a romantic fairy tale, but it was a true story of real people, an immigrant family led by the milkmaid and the hired hand from Tåstorp, in pursuit of a dream apparently fulfilled but later shattered by the horrific deaths of too many loved ones. Even so, should they have remained in Sweden? What if they had never pursued their dream? Their legacy in this country is much larger than their tombstone. Their descendants are many, and we who have heard their story marvel at what they did.

Johannes and Kristina Lundborg

Johannes, Kristina, and Andrew made Carver County their home, eventually purchased farmland, and settled there to raise a family with 11 more children.

Johannes did become part of the Union Army before the Civil War ended. Records tell us he served in Company "A" of the 11th Regiment of the Minnesota Volunteer Infantry. He was recruited in August 1864, and the regiment left Fort Snelling September 20 for Nashville, Tennesee. Kristina, five months pregnant with Charlotte, was left on the farm with 2-year-old Andrew. Andreas and Lena were nearby with Johanna and Samuel to offer their support during some of Johannes' absence.

The duty of Company A was to guard important sections of the Louisville and Nashville Railroad, which was head-quartered in Gallatin. They performed numerous scouting expeditions on the trail of guerilla bands that were raiding throughout that area. It is said there were frequent exciting incidents, an occasional encounter that gave promise of a respectable fight, but little heavy action. In one of those encounters two members of the regiment were killed. The members of the 11th regiment were relieved of their service June 25 and ordered back to Minnesota where they were mustered out July 11, 1865. The very patriotic communities of East Union and West Union, named to honor the Union Army, were proud and relieved to see their young men return home. (This information is from *Minnesota in Three Centuries, Vol. 3,* an old book by Warren Upham, originally written in 1908 and recently re-published.) Johannes was now almost 33 years old, his family tragedy and military service were behind him, and he was ready to fulfill his Swedish dream of operating his own farm and raising a family.

And did they ever raise a family! In the 24 years between 1862 and 1886 Kristina bore 12 children. Alfred, born in 1884, was the only child to perish in childhood, and Elfrida died at 21. Two of their sons moved to the east coast, four settled in northern Minnesota, and the others remained in Carver County or nearby. Family members busied themselves in work on the farm and were involved in the church. Johannes, who was a deacon in the West Lake Church, was known as a good Bible teacher and scholar at West Union. Old pictures of the home they lived in reveal a big house with a large, open front porch suitable for the gatherings of a large family.

In 1894 Johannes qualified for a disability pension. His application indicates his health deteriorated in his later years due to a condition he incurred during the war. He noted pains in his chest and side that made it difficult for him to work on the farm. Johannes died November 15, 1899 at 67 and is buried at West Union. Kristina lived until November 6, 1901 and died young, at 57. She is buried beside Johannes.

Sarah Lundborg Lundquist

She has not been mentioned often, but she also belongs to the list of survivors. She was the daughter who remained in Sweden. On August 20, 1862 she probably had a very busy day caring for her 2-year-old daughter Selma and Gustaf, her 9-month-old son. She and her husband Johannes were working together in the Lundquist Store they owned in Vårgårda, a store destined to have a long life from 1860 until 1895 when it burned, and came to life again after a year. It would take months for a letter to reach Sweden to inform her of her brothers' deaths, and she would then be an "old" 19-year-old wife, mother, storekeeper, and bereft sister. Were there grief-stricken letters between her and her parents, or did they each quietly feel their loss in private moments and shelter it deep in their souls? No records exist to inform us. Thankfully, she had uncles, aunts, and cousins with whom she could share memories and her sorrow.

In addition to running the store she and her husband raised eleven children. Several of their children came to America to settle permanently, and only in recent years have the American Lundborgs and Lundquists come to know of each other. Sarah died May 26, 1907. She was not an eyewitness to the tragedy; nonetheless she was a survivor living a long distance from the rest of her family.

Johanna Lundborg Paulson

After returning to West Lake in 1865 Johanna went to school in St. Cloud, returned home, and married Erick Paulson in 1869. She was able to cross a formidable boundary by marrying a Norwegian, and they settled on the original Lundborg property to raise their six children. Johanna died March 21, 1916 and is buried at West Norway Lake Lutheran Church cemetery Sunburg, Minnesota, and Erick died June 4, 1921. Paulsons continue to this day to live on the land first settled in 1861.

Samuel Lundborg

Samuel returned to Carver County with his father and farmed there the rest of his life. He married Anna Maria Johnson, and they raised six children. It was said he carried a bullet in his side all through the rest of his life and suffered from it. His name was honored as it was passed on to Johannes' third son and to August's son, Sigfrid—my father—for whom it was a second name. Samuel died May 23, 1920 at 67 and is buried at the West Union Cemetery. Anna died Jan. 24, 1916 at 61.

Peter Broberg

Peter Broberg, the little boy who interrupted the service August 20, 1862 and was the single survivor of his family, married Christina Larson Dec. 31, 1878.

Growing up in New London he enjoyed a variety of summer jobs that led to his recognition as a good worker. In a small community that is a most admirable trait, and Peter went on to become a successful businessman. The Swenson and Broberg Store was theirs. He and Christina raised four children. Before his death in 1925 he erected a small monument to his family members killed in 1862. His touching tribute stands in Monson Lake State Park to this day, and its misspellings testify to its very personal and heartfelt nature. He didn't ask a committee to proofread. "This [imm]emorial [err]ected by P. Broberg being one of the remnants of the massacre. June 1, 1917." He died Dec. 28, 1925 at the age of 71.

Anna Stina Broberg

After 1925 she was the last of the family witnesses alive. Anna Stina Broberg married John Peterson on September 10, 1864 at Nest Lake, where they farmed. In 1880 they moved to St. Hilaire in northern Minnesota where they also farmed. They had six children, and the family was active in the Swedish Lutheran Church. In 1927 the Monson Lake Memorial Association held their first event to commemorate the lives of the Brobergs and Lundborgs who were killed in 1862, and

Anna Stina returned to the area to be a guest speaker. She was able to attend several other commemorative events. She died Sept. 12, 1933 at the age of 87. She and her husband are both buried in St. Hilaire, MN.

And here ends the story of the first generation of the survivors. Did they talk to one another about this story? Were they eager to tell others? Was it too painful, so they kept the story to themselves? A book first published in 1864 contains a two page account of what took place August 20, 1862, attributed to 16-year-old Anna Stina Broberg. Through the years she must have continued to talk about it enough that she was interviewed, and her later written account is well known. She lived long enough to participate in public remembrances of the event. Our Swedish ancestors have a reputation for handling suffering in a stoic manner. Is that what they did? Peter put up a small monument, and Anna Stina's story is written, but that is all the tangible testimony we have from the survivors. The oral tradition has weakened through the generations, so today's descendants are thankful Peter and Anna Stina left some kind of record of their memories of this tragedy.

Thanks be to God for their lives, for their survival that enabled other generations to come to life, and for every little bit of information that has given us a glimpse of who they were.

Chapter Nine

꩜

The Following Generations

Here I'll pick up the genealogical overview of those who came after Johannes, and narrow the scope to lead to my immediate family.

6th Generation

Johannes and Kristina Lundborg had 12 children, and most all of their years they lived on a farm in Carver County.

Andrew (Anders) Lundborg (9/20/1862 in Afton, Minnesota to 1/29/1936 in Worcester, Massachusets.) He married Hilda Ekendahl in 1901, and they had one daughter, Alfhild Marie. Andrew graduated from Augustana College in Rock Island, IL and moved to Worcester in 1889 where he owned a jewelry store, was active in local politics and in his church. He was 73 when he died.

Charlotte E. (Lotte) Lundborg (1/31/1865–11/25/1948) 83 years. Born on the family farm in Carver County she married John Ahlin Anderson, and they lived and farmed mostly in Isanti County where they are buried. They had six children. I have recently met one of her grandchildren, 89-year-old Donald Honebrink, who lives in Seattle along with a number of other distant members of the Lundborg clan.

August Lundborg (3/24/1867–10/13/1939) 72 years. He was my grandfather and died four years before I was born. He married **Anna Wahlstrom** (1/31/1869–4/7/1960) in Carver County. Both were born in West Union, and both are buried at Stockholm Lutheran Church Cemetery in Wright County, not far from their farm near Cokato. They had ten children, and seven survived into adulthood. Both were musicians and very active in their church life. Anna's half brother Matthias Wahlstrom was an early president of Gustavus College. Her uncle was Peter Carlson, a pastor who helped establish the Augustana Synod and who was a dear friend of Andrew Jackson. August was in the US Cavalry stationed at Yellowstone Park and upon returning to Minnesota, he and Anna lived on a series of farms in northern Minnesota before buying a farm near Cokato sold to them by Kristina's (Mrs. Johannes Lundborg) sister.

Samuel P. Lundborg (7/10/1870–12/2/1942) 72 years. He was born in Carver County, moved east to be near his brother Andrew for a while, returned to the Midwest to purchase and run a jewelry store in Brainerd, Minnesota for many years. In 1913 he married Selma Louisa Liljedahl (1876–?) who was born in Sweden. Their one child, Margaret, continued to run the store after her father died.

Johanna Lundborg (1872–1950) never married during her 78 year lifetime.

John A. Lundborg (9/26/1874–10/15/1949) 75 years. He was born in Carver County, married Emma Schwanenberg (1873–1924), a German, Dec. 22, 1903. They had one son Carl. Emma died young at 51, and John remarried, but I have no record. His farm was near the farm run by his sister Charlotte and her husband, but John died in Crow Wing County, perhaps while visiting other siblings who lived near Nisswa. He is buried in Belle Plaine, MN.

Anna Lundborg (12/15/1876–10/25/1959) 82 years.

Theodore A. Lundborg (3/17/1879–11/8/1960) 81 years.

Joseph Lundborg (8/1885–12/16/1954) 69 years.

These siblings sound like colorful personalities. Notes from cousin Dick about Theodore, Joseph and Anna: "Theodore, Joseph and Anna lived together near Nisswa, MN. They ran a nursery, a fruit farm and raised mink. Joseph did considerable "leg" work fighting US Government water policies (i.e. dam and/or drainage projects) that affected their property. Joseph may have attended Gustavus Adolphus College for a while. He started a short-lived newspaper at one time. After Joseph and Anna died, Theodore was cared for by Margaret (Lundborg) Larson (Samuel's daughter) in Brainerd. Anna died in the hospital in Cambridge, MN; Theodore died in the hospital in Park Rapids, MN; and Joseph died in the hospital in St. Cloud, MN. The three are buried in the Nisswa Cemetery. The graves are marked by individual flat stones and lie under several large spruce trees in the upper left quarter of the cemetery."

Esther Lundborg (1879–1949) 75 years. She is buried in the East Union Cemetery. Cousin Dick's notes indicate she and her sister Johanna spent some time in mental hospitals.

Elfrida Lundborg (3/26/1886–3/24/1908) 21 years. From cousin Dick: Elfrida studied nursing at Bethesda Hospital in St. Paul, MN. She was engaged to a Rev. Nystrom, but died of scarlet fever before she finished her training. She is buried at the West Union Lutheran Church Cemetery.

Alfred Lundborg. Recent information has come to light of a son named Alfred born to Johannes and Kristina, but information is incomplete. Born sometime around 1874 and died before 1880.

At this time less is known about this generation than about the two generations born before them. Perhaps more discoveries will be made in the future. Of the 12 children born to Johannes and Kristina, only five married, and the following generation numbered only 16—seven for August, one for Andrew, one for Samuel, one for John, and six for Charlotte.

7th Generation

My grandparents, **August and Anna Lundborg**, had ten children altogether, and seven survived into adulthood. Three sets of twins were born to them.

Albin Lundborg (5/3/1897–5/28/1971) 74 years. Born in West Union, he was with his parents on the home farm in Carver County, the adventures in three different communities in northern Minnesota, and finally in Cokato where they purchased their own farm and settled there. He never married, so he continued to live with his parents. After his dad's death in 1939 he ran the farm, and it was sold after his mother's death in 1960.

Edith and Amy Lundborg (twins) were born in 1899 and died at six weeks of pneumonia.

Sigfrid Samuel Lundborg and Edwin Emanuel Lundborg were fraternal twins born March 27, 1901, in West Union. Sig, my father died July 15, 1954 at the age of 53, and Uncle Eddie died November 25, 1984 at the age of 83. Eddie farmed near Dassell, not far from the family farm near Cokato, and Sig was an entrepreneurial butter maker who owned three businesses—creamery, chicken hatchery, and meat locker plant, plus raised turkeys—before his early death. Eddie died at Dassell, and Sig died in Montevideo, MN, near his home in Milan. Eddie married Ruth Hagstrom, and they had two sons. Sig married Frances Ronning, and they had four children.

Amy Lundborg Danielson (3/13/1903–3/21/1999) 96 years. She was born in Brunswick, MN, when the family worked in northern Minnesota. This was the pre-Cokato era. She worked as a teacher and farmer's wife. She married Arvid Danielson (1908–?), and they farmed near TriMont, MN. They had two sons. Amy was a great story-teller, and she was the one who first told me the family story about August 20, 1862. I'm sorry that it was not until I was 38 years old that I first heard it, but I'm eternally grateful for hearing Aunt Amy's version.

Edith Lundborg Mattson (4/29/1905–3/13/1966) 60 years. She was born in Isanti County in northern Minnesota and had a twin sister who was stillborn. She married Art Mattson and they lived in the Park Rapids, MN, area. They raised two sons.

Alice Lundborg McGuire (10/4/1907–6/5/1990) 82 years. Her birthplace is Day, MN, which is in the same area as Brunswick in northern Minnesota. She was a nurse, married Charles (Uncle Charlie) McGuire, who worked for the railroad. They lived in the Twin Cities and in Nisswa, MN, after retirement. They raised two sons also. A pattern?

Oscar Oliver (Uncle Pat) Lundborg (10/1/1912) 85 years. He was born in Braham, MN. August and Anna lived and worked near three towns in Isanti County—Brunswick, Day, and Braham—and managed to claim each of those communities as a birth place for at least one of their children. Pat married Florence Huseby, and they raised four children—two sons and two daughters. He worked as a musician all over the Midwest and in various agriculture-related activities in Milan and Madison, MN. He was a fine athlete—very good baseball player and lifelong golfer. There were musical gifts aplenty in the descendants of August and Anna, and Uncle Pat's trumpet was a treat to hear.

8th generation

This is the generation I was born into, the descendants of **Sig and Frances (Ronning) Lundborg.** My dad left the family farm near Cokato when he was 14 years old because times were tough and he picked up on the subtle message that "someone needs to leave if we're all going to eat." He quit school and hired out to neighboring farmers so he could have a small salary and a place to live. When the time was right, he was trained as a butter maker, and that gave him a skill to sell. He worked in a number of small communities in Minnesota, came to the Montevideo area, met my mother—an 18-year-old telephone operator—and married her. Opportunity knocked, and he bought the creamery in Milan early in the 1940's, and that's where they settled. He was a hard-working, enterprising businessman in a small town, and his life was cut short by a heart weakened from a childhood bout with rheumatic fever. He died in 1954 during a "minor" surgical procedure.

Robert Francis Lundborg (9/7/1929–9/29/1999) 70 years. Bob was born in Montevideo, spent some time at Gustavus, the US Army (in Germany during the Korean War), and at the University of Minnesota. He left school to run the family business when Sig died. After a number of years in business, he made a successful transition into the world of insurance sales and worked for Lutheran Brotherhood Insurance. He married Nancy Verna Haverick in 1954, and they raised four children. Both Bob and Nancy suffered from health issues, and Bob received a transplanted new heart in 1994 that gave him an extra five years.

We three younger siblings are Janet Long (born 2/6/1932), Nancy Ann Lundborg (born 12/11/1939), and Paul (born

10/26/1943). Janet and Nancy both worked as nurses, and I was a Lutheran pastor.

9th & 10th & 11th generations

We have now come to the 9th and 10th generations after Torsten Algottson's 1712 beginnings. The year of this writing—2012—marks 300 years since patriarch Torsten's birth, and the 1862 war and family tragedy split those three centuries in half. My wife, Rose Ann, and I have two married sons and two granddaughters who, at the time of this writing, are 3 and 9. At this time also there are many grandchildren born to my siblings, and the first member of the 11th generation in our part of the whole clan was born in 2012.

In future years someone will dig deeper into our history and learn far more than anyone knows right now. And in future years more generations will be born and the branches of the family tree will spread. Surely, anyone who researches the Lundborg or Broberg genealogy will stop and linger awhile in the year 1862 and will wonder what might have been if . . . I've done my share of wondering, and it's been interesting at best, but far more fruitful have been the times of marveling that those of us who are here, are here. It might have been that no one survived that day, or that no one even witnessed what happened. Some survived. The story was remembered. We are here, and we have the story. That's good enough for me.

Chapter Ten

❧

The Role of Religion

I am by nature and training curious about God and religion in all aspects of human life. So when I reflect on my family's origins, the story of their daily lives, the drama of leaving home and beginning anew, their meeting with a new race and culture, the struggle for land, the tragedy of war and grief, and the slow path towards healing and reconciliation, I can't help myself. I wonder about issues of personal faith, institutionalized Christianity, comparative religions, contrasting theological perspectives. I get headaches when I do all of this at once, and I try to not be terribly dogmatic about what I say, but something would be missing if I said nothing about this topic.

To this point I have noticed my family's deep roots in Lutheran Christianity. It would have been impossible to miss this basic point. I have introduced their pastor into this narrative and mentioned the family's participation in congregational life. Examining any tragedy can draw many of us closer to contemplating our own mortality, and for many that means facing what I would loosely call God questions. So here are assorted observations on the significance of religion in this story.

Andreas and Lena Lundborg, born in 1812 and 1810 respectively, were baptized into a Lutheran Church that was an arm of their government. Lutheranism began in Germany in 1517 and within 20 years was institutionalized in many parts of Scandinavia. Roman Catholicism was displaced, and Rome no longer held power among most of Sweden's faithful. The content of the faith and its significant practices were changed, but the administration of that faith remained a top-down affair with religion and government together wielding power over the common person.

Faith was certainly still a personal matter, and levels of devotion differed, but I am struck by the church's efforts to control the populace. Remember the detailed church records? Recall the "exit interview" with the parish pastor? The requirement to meet with the pastor before leaving the country and enduring the pastor's questioning and evaluation resembled a permission-asking experience. Would anyone today be willing to be subject to such churchly authority? We know church participation as a voluntary experience, and it would be ludicrous even to imagine such authoritative muscle being exerted by any Lutheran pastor or congregation today. Today's Lutheran church, or any denomination's church, has little or no authority over individual's lives in today's world, especially in America. The pope and the Roman Catholic bishops think they have the power to control, but American Catholicism contains many independent thinkers.

Nineteenth century Scandinavians immigrating to America looked for freedom from oppressive religious leaders. But at the same time as they fled religion's authority, our ancestors craved religion's structure. Early efforts to Americanize Swedish Lutheranism were resisted. Immigrant pastors from the old country hung on to their old ways. Perhaps the only missing item in pastoral practice was the paycheck from the government, and that might have been a key to whatever modest innovation took place, but I'm struck by how our Swedish ancestors spent so much time in church organization, constitution-writing, and fighting turf wars with other denominations and other language groups. They were doing what was necessary to survive, but the patterns they set in place held power in American Lutheranism for a long time. I believe that same power is felt even today. Maybe what I'm observing is that it has taken a long time to forget that we are no longer part of a state church.

There are two stories of 19th century Minnesota Christians who were not afraid of the Indians, who sought to know them, who attempted to build relationships with them, and these people were not Lutherans. Perhaps there were many more, but they aren't well known.

In the early 1800's a physician who was the son of a Presbyterian pastor came to the area very near where I was born and lived my first 18 years. Dr. Thomas Williamson came to Lac Qui Parle (French for "Lake who speaks"), a wide spot on the Minnesota River not very far from Milan, to a trading post run by Joseph Renville to begin a mission school. For nearly 20 years—1835–1854—Williamson with the help of various assistants led an effort to educate and evangelize the Dakota people who lived in the area. If the success of this venture were measured by numbers of converts, it was a failure. But relationships were established and nurtured. Some intermarrying took place. White people took an interest in Dakota people, even learned to speak their language, sing their songs, and worked with the Dakota language enough to translate the Bible into Dakota. Two hundred years earlier the French traders and trappers learned how to work with the Dakota people, but the British and American settlers were not so adept. Williamson and his partners invested their lives in the Dakota people. They might not have respected the Dakota religion. They might have viewed them as "pagans" or "heathens," but their commitment to live among and work with the Dakota was an admirable trait. William-son later moved to near Granite Falls and worked among the Indians living at the Upper Agency. Stephen Riggs was one of his early assistants at the mission and shared the same commitment to this mission among the Dakota. Later, how-ever, many Dakota belt betrayed by Riggs in his work as a translator at the trials beginning at Camp Release. Wil-liamson braved the anti-Indian sentiment of 1862 to criticize Riggs for "succumbing to the biased atmosphere of the mili-tary camp." (*North Country: The Making of Minnesota.* Mary Wingerd. University of Minnesota Press, 2010) Williamson's work was exemplary.

In 1859 Rev. Henry Whipple was elected bishop of Min-nesota's Episcopal Church, an office he held until his death in 1901. He was born in upstate New York and served con-gregations there and in Chicago before coming west to the new state. He was a high church Episcopalian but was drawn to minister to those who lived on the margins of society, and he spent time with both the Dakota and Ojibwe people prior to becoming a bishop. One historian says Whipple was the most unpopular man in Minnesota because of his advocat-ing on behalf of the Dakota at the conclusion of the war in 1862. According to the newly written *North Country: The Making of Minnesota,* Whipple was targeted with death threats because he interceded with President Lincoln, begging him to not put to death the 303 Dakota sentenced to be hanged. He also pleaded that Lincoln not banish the Dakota from the state. His influence with the President was significant because Lincoln pardoned all but 38, and many feared the state's hatred would erupt. Evidently, the decision to ban-ish the Indians calmed enough vengeance-filled hearts to at least temporarily settle the storm of the war's aftermath.

Whipple's quest for justice towards the Indian stands out in its near solitude as a voice among Christian leaders of the time. Would any president other than the compassionate

Lincoln have listened to him? Why no other champions for social justice? Why the easy acceptance of "eye for an eye" morality in the churches?

I found references to efforts to raise funds for displaced settlers in the Lutheran church meetings of 1862, prayers for strength and healing for families of the victims, but no prayers for the Indians, no voices urging moderation. I say this not in the spirit of "I would have done better." I can't imagine what I would have done as a pastor in that impossible situation. I know that fearful people caught up in the urgency of survival issues will have no desire to love their enemy. Horrific crimes were committed against innocents, so there was reason to hate. But some Christian leaders did not hate. Williamson and Whipple were brave souls, compassionate people. Why were Lutheran clergy of that day not able or willing to work alongside Williamson and Whipple? Perhaps this is an unfair question, but I will raise it anyway. I believe the Swedes lived too long in a system that tied church and state together. The government was no longer running their church, but the immigrants' dated worldview limited their perspective. It is difficult, at best, for a state-run church to have a sense of mission. It is next to impossible for a state-run church to criticize the government. It is not realistic for a state-run church to call for justice towards the enemy of the state. Churches in America certainly were not state run in 1862 nor are they now, but among Lutherans there is still a reluctance to quarrel with the government, and I'm persuaded that is due to our deep roots in an old system.

The absence of a prophetic message, a social conscience, and a desire to welcome the stranger are marks of a church that is linked with the powers that be. Our Swedish Lutheran ancestry has continued to influence Lutheranism even today. We have been slow to criticize government, to care for the poor and needy, and to be welcoming towards those who are different from us. I say this not to be scornful of our ancestors but instead to be understanding of why they responded to their tense situation as they did. I understand better why it has not been easy for Lutherans to have embraced the quest for civil rights for all, why there have not been many conscientious objectors among Lutheran people, why we have been stand-offish towards those of other religions. Our roots are deep and powerful.

Not all Christians are alike. It's not that Williamson and Whipple were right and Jackson, Carlson, and Norelius wrong. They were each being who they were, responding to how they were shaped, and my understanding of why the Lutheran cries for befriending the Dakota were few and far between has deepened.

Which makes me wonder: how will our descendants, 150 years from now, look back on us and wonder what our Christian witness was? Will we still be writing church constitutions, breaking away from one congregation and starting new ones, separating ourselves from those who think differently than we do? I don't have any magic prescriptions for what will help us embody the Bible's teachings of Jesus, and I don't want this to become a sermon. But I want to raise the question: Why were there no voices like Williamson's and Whipple's among 19th century Lutherans? Will our descendants look back and discover any such voices among us 21st century Lutherans? What other conspicuous absences might the future generations note concerning the practice of our faith?

And if my question offends, I close with an apology. I shouldn't assume all who read this will worry and wonder about the Lutheran Christian faith our ancestors practiced. Not all of today's generations profess a faith at all, and certainly those who practice a faith that is part of mainline denominational Christianity are in a minority. Others might not like the question. But it's who I am, as my ancestors were being who they were. True to my Swedish origins I raise my questions respectfully, quietly, and cautiously.

Chapter Eleven

❧

The Story Lives

As a 6th grader in school in Milan, Minnesota I remember we studied Minnesota history and even visited the state capitol. If Minnesota schools still teach the story of the Dakota/US War of 1862, many Minnesotans have heard of governmental leaders like Governor Alexander Ramsey and General Henry Sibley; religious leaders like Bishop Whipple, and missionaries Dr. Thomas Williamson and Steven Riggs; and Indian leaders like Little Crow and Big Eagle. The story of the Brobergs, Lundborgs, and Pastor Jackson is known only to a few. Their names are not familiar to many. It isn't necessary to name governmental and political leaders in their story, and we don't know the names of any of the Indians who were there at Monson Lake that day. Not until recently have I had the chance to talk to any Dakota people about my ancestors, but now I can at least make a somewhat indirect connection to the name of one Dakota warrior.

I've told the story of our ancestors to a number of people through the years, and it always evokes a strong response. Here's my account of the most memorable time, when I told it to a Dakota man, and I wrote this in 1983 shortly after my meeting with him. Try to appreciate the timing of this writing—nearly 30 years ago—and that this was one of my first steps in learning the family story by trying to tell it to someone else.

(Parenthetical comment: I sold this writing to the magazine *The Lutheran Standard,* a journal of the American Lutheran Church. They paid me $40 and never published it. I don't know why.)

Coincidence? Providence? I still don't know what to call it. There is meaning to it. The kind of meaning that tingles my spine and moistens my eye. The kind of meaning whose full significance I yet can't grasp.

There was this conference. The title of the event was "One in the Spirit." Arranged by Native Americans. Sponsored by several groups, one of which was the National Indian Lutheran Board. Small group. Limited to 50 participants. One third Indian. Aimed at Lutheran clergy, the purpose of the event was to communicate Indian spirituality to white Christian leaders.

The event attracted me. Midwestern Lutheran romantic that I am I have been reading about Indians for the past few years. It probably all started with Bury My Heart at Wounded Knee. *Hit its peak with* Hanta-Yo *and even led me to pursue my illusions far enough to plan and begin to build a tipi. There's something about the literature and the heritage of the plains Indians that fascinated me.*

Two years ago, 1981, I learned that my family history is intimately tied to that of Midwestern Indians through a conflict earlier historians called the last Sioux Uprising, and it occurred in 1862 in Minnesota. My great grandfather, Johannes Lundborg, and four of his brothers left a church service to check out a story about hostile actions on the part of Sioux Indians near their rough cabin by Sunburg, Minnesota. Three of his brothers were killed, and another was wounded. Ten other relatives were also killed. If Johannes had not survived, I wouldn't be here. Many on both sides were wounded or killed. The warfare was concluded by the hanging of 38 Sioux men by the US government.

I'm thankful for great grandfather Johannes. And I'm thankful for the richness of Indian history that has informed me. Thankful enough to attend this conference called "One in the Spirit." At this event I shared my family story with Gene Crawford. He's the executive director of the National Indian Lutheran Board. He's a Dakota Indian, what I used to know as "Sioux." His family has roots in South Dakota. I told him my story—great grandfather Johannes, etc. He told me his. His great grandfather was one of the 38 who were hanged.

There he and I were. A couple of Lutheran Christians. We're at this conference for different reasons. He's a pro with a job to do. I'm an idealistic pastor grabbed by a story about my family. He's Indian. I'm not. Four generations before us our families were at war with each other. "One in the Spirit" wasn't on their minds. Land, treaties, safety, survival—that's what they dealt with. I'm glad I live now. I'm thankful for my heritage. I like Gene Crawford. He's thankful for his heritage. We have more things in common. One in the Spirit? Yes. There's something bigger than both of us that brought us together. Don't you think?

Who was Eugene Crawford? Gene (1928–1986) was a Dakota Indian (Sisseton) raised on the Lake Traverse Reservation who became the first and only executive director of the National Indian Lutheran Board, formed in 1970 and no longer existing. He was the son of a Presbyterian clergyman and served as executive director of the American Indian Center in Omaha before joining the Lutheran Council in the USA. Leaders of the former American Lutheran Church said Crawford was the catalyst for Lutheran American Indian ministry. An advocate for Native American Indian causes, Crawford served as a mediator at the Wounded Knee and Alcatraz occupations in the mid-1970s. Though not a Lutheran when he began work with the NILB, he became a Lutheran prior to his death in 1986, because of the commitment of Lutherans to ministry with American Indians. And also, he told me, because of his beautiful Danish Lutheran wife.

Eugene and I corresponded briefly after the conference in 1983, and his wife sent a note in 1986 informing me of his death. In recent years as I have read more about the Dakota/US War, I have wondered about Gene's great grandfather. In recent writings the 38 who were hanged are named, but I've never known which one was related to Gene—until recently, July 13, 2012. A telephone conversation with a Lutheran bishop in southwestern Minnesota led me to a Lakota Lutheran man who directed me to a Dakota teacher living on the Lake Traverse Reservation in South Dakota who knew Eugene. Several months ago this man (Danny Seaboy) attended the funeral of Eugene's brother who died at 103 years of age. When I asked if he knew the name of Gene's great grandfather, the response was quick. "Chaska," he said. Pronounced "Chas-kay," not like Chaska, the county seat of Carver County. Following the mass execution on December 26, a mistake was discovered. Wicaŋhpi Wastedaŋpi (We-chank-wash-ta-don-pee), who went by the common name of Caske (meaning first-born son), reportedly stepped forward when the name "Caske" was called, and was then separated for execution from the other prisoners.

There was another Chaska who should have been put to death; however, this Chaska should never have been hanged. That could probably be said of many of the 38 because the trials barely resembled a formal legal process. 303 Dakota were initially sentenced to death, but President Lincoln pardoned most all of them. Chaska was pardoned, but his hanging, some say, was a case of mistaken identity. Chaska was the rescuer of Sarah Wakefield, and in her book she says he treated her kindly. Others say the guards believed Chaska was Wakefield's secret lover and deserved to die, so there was no accident. There are efforts today to give Chaska a posthumous pardon, and perhaps that process would open the files of all the others to publicly evaluate how fair these trials were. Chaska's story reveals one insight into the many tales of deep suffering the Dakota experienced. And he is the reminder ours was not the only innocent family hurt by the 1862 tragedy.

Broberg, Lundborg, Crawford, Chaska. Stories told of the personalities of history who are bigger than life are interesting to read, but they remain "out there," distant. Find out you're a blood relative, or friend of a blood relative, and you're hooked. When the story comes closer, its meaning can change. I know a descendant of one of the 38 who were hanged, and my understanding of who he was and they were is now different. Maybe the story sounds different to you, if you know me.

The story of my ancestors is alive and well, deep within my soul. It's one part of an important piece of history in Sweden and in Minnesota. I'm a descendant of Swedish immigrants who had big dreams and suffered a huge tragedy. Perhaps every human who has walked on this earth has known similar hopes and despair, but knowing this story to be true about my relatives makes it different. Think of the countless victims of wars through the centuries. My family is now connected to those stories of suffering.

Is it because I didn't know it as a child and intuitively sensed something was missing? Is it because my dad died when I was young and I've had such minimal contact with Lundborg relatives over the years? Whatever the reasons, this story is important to me.

Lutheran pastor and theologian Dietrich Bonhoeffer helps to explain the meaning of significant losses in life and uses the image of a "protected emptiness" to describe what it is like to experience grief. When we lose someone we love, he counsels to not try to fill up the empty place but to protect it. Bonhoeffer says, "It is nonsense to say that God fills the gap; God does not fill it, but on the contrary, keeps it empty and so helps us to keep alive our former communion with each other, even at the cost of pain." (*Letters and Papers from Prison*)

This protected emptiness within has led me to learn about and have communion with Torsten Algottson and all his descendants, especially Andreas and Lena and their offspring. They led me to the Brobergs and Bengt Andreasson and Jerker Saxentorp and Lia Detterfelt and all those relatives in Sweden. And Paulsons and Lundquists and other Lundborgs I've not yet met. Pastor Jackson and the churches in Kandiyohi County and Carver County. And John Knife Sterner, Danny Seaboy, Gene Crawford and Chaska. And you, reading these pages. The circle is growing wider, and it's time to end my writing, and I am led to what is a frequent saying of the Dakota people. "Mitakuye Oyasin"—we are all related. All, my relatives. What a gift! Thanks be to God!

May there be others in the family whose curiosity leads them to correct the mistakes, fill in the blanks, and gather new information. May honoring our ancestors bring us closer together and give us a new appreciation for what it means to belong to a family.

Chapter Twelve

ℰℐℴ

Epilogue

The year 2012 is significant for the Lundborgs. It marks 300 years since the birth of Torsten Algottson, the essential patriarch of the Lundborg clan. He is worthy of that title because thus far there is nothing available to document his ancestors. He is as far back as we go. And 2012 is being commemorated as the Sesquicentennial of the US/Dakota War of 1862. That year was the halfway mark in the three centuries of my family's known history, and was marked by a great tragedy. Certainly, 2012 should be an appropriate time to bring together as many of the descendants of the survivors as possible in an effort to express gratitude for their survival and hope for the future. With no mailing list to work from, a small cadre of four people came together a year in advance to set aside the dates of August 18 and 19, 2012 for a gathering. "Honoring Our Ancestors: A Gathering for Descendants of the Survivors—Brobergs, Lundborgs, Paulsons, and Lundquists"—that was our theme. 150 came together including 17 from Sweden to meet and greet and to recall the family story. They met initially at Monson Lake State Park near Sunburg on a beautiful late summer day. The site includes the marker for the Broberg cabins built in 1861 and a monument erected by Peter Broberg in 1925.

The site is where the killings happened and where the bodies were buried until 1891 when they were moved to New London. There was an opportunity to visit the Paulson farm which is where a marker for the Lundborg cabin is located, and many drove by to view a site close to where the Isle of Refuge was located in Norway Lake. A Scandinavian meal was served at Peace Lutheran Church in New London where all could visit the monument in the cemetery and also visit the displays of the Monongalia County Historical Society located in the old Lebanon Lutheran Church building. I am so thankful for that day together and gratified to have met many new relatives.

On Sunday the members of the Norway Lake Lutheran Historical Association hosted a worship gathering at the site of the old log church in the country near to First Lutheran Church of Norway Lake. I was invited to be the guest preacher for the occasion, and here is what I said on that day.

SERMON: "Remembering and Forgetting"
Norway Lake Lutheran Historical Church
Pennock, Minnesota
August 19, 2012

God's Beloved People:

Grace to you and peace. Thank you for inviting me to be your preacher this day as you come together to celebrate your 13th anniversary service at this replica of the original Old Log Church. And your special service coincides with Minnesota's commemoration of the 150th anniversary of the Dakota/US War of 1862. That war's impact was felt locally with the deaths of 20 residents in this area, and it gets personalized because 13 of those victims were my relatives who had recently come from Sweden to settle in the West Lake area, which is now known as Monson Lake. My great grandfather's three brothers were killed August 20, 1862, not too far from here, along with ten other family members.

Yesterday a group of what we have called "descendants of the survivors" met together at Monson Lake State Park and Peace Lutheran Church in New London in a first-time family reunion event in order to honor our ancestors.

With that much history on our minds this is a good day for the preacher to focus on a theme related to remembering and forgetting—for this is what we always do with history. I will read a text from the prophet Isaiah, the 43rd chapter, selected verses where God speaks comfort to those who have suffered:

"Do not fear, for I have redeemed you; I have called you by name, you are mine. When you pass through the waters, I will be with you, and through the rivers, they shall not overwhelm you. Because you are precious in my sight, and honored, and I love you....Do not fear. For I am with you.

Do not remember the former things, or consider the things of old. I am about to do a new thing; now it springs forth, do you not perceive it? I, I am He who blots out your transgressions for my own sake, and I will not remember your sins."

I am now of an age where it's dangerous to talk about remembering and forgetting. We have our funny moments at home—the keys, the phone, the remote, the glasses. Where did I put them? I saw old "what's-his-name" today. You know who I mean.Forgetting is so easy.

I love a poem by Billy Collins entitled "Forgetfulness." It's so true and so funny that I decided to memorize it. But I couldn't. Remembering is hard work.

I grew up not too far from here in Milan. I spent my first 18 years there, and I'm thankful for my Milan roots. I don't get there as often anymore since we live out in Washington state where we've been now for 30 years, but in the years when I would return to Milan more frequently the same thing would always happen to me. I could not visit Milan and live in the present tense. In every visit I would feel like I was caught in a time warp. I was so caught up in "remembering when" that the nostalgia would feel suffocating. Too much remembering wasn't such a good experience.

Even in your presence today, even though I've not been to your church before, I'm remembering two people I associate with you. Rev. John Victor Halvorson was one of my favorite teachers from Luther Seminary in St. Paul, MN, and he came from here. His grandfather was a pastor here. Rev. Ron Burke was a pastor here who moved to Milan, and he became a friend while he cared for my mother and brother and other family members during his pastoral work in Milan.

At any one moment in life we feel the tug of the past—good memories and not so good ones; the pull of the future—what we desire, what we fear. And whenever those forces consume us, we fail to live in this present moment.

Why would we ever want to remember the bad things? I've had to answer that question often lately as I've told friends I'm going to Minnesota to commemorate the 150th anniversary of a war where 13 of my relatives were killed. "Why?," many asked. It's not easy to answer with a few words. Why remember the Dakota/US War of 1862 and the deaths of my family members?

1. One reason: I don't want to risk forgetting them. I didn't know the story of the Lundborgs and Brobergs and the 13 tragic deaths until I was 38 years old. I was shocked to hear it! But I've savored it over the years. The story has given me a glimpse into the lives of my family members. Until I was in my late 30's my only awareness of ancestors was that my dad's family came from Sweden and my mom's family came from Norway. At a hastily arranged extended family gathering on September 12, 1981 near Madison my aunt Amy—my dad's sister—started talking about the Indians who killed her grandpa's brothers, and I thought she was

teasing. That was a life-changing moment for me to begin to learn a foundational story about my ancestors. My grandfathers died before I was born, my father died entirely too young, so I didn't get to hear this story. Still, it has remained alive among a few historians, scattered family members, in this community, and in Sweden, Now, it's important to me. I don't want to forget the victims—my family.

And it's a delicate matter to not forget them. To remember my relatives I end up reminding all who listen of an event in Minnesota history that invites sorrow, anger, guilt, shame. Who wouldn't be angry at those who brought suffering and death to their family members?

In 1862 there was lots of anger. Among the Dakota people there was anger at the whites for taking their land, for breaking the treaties, for failing to provide the promised money and food, for taking away their culture, language, religion, and traditions. When their anger erupted, the settlers were fearful and even more angry. Angry enough to banish all Dakota people from the state. Angry enough to thoroughly demean and dehumanize all Indians for decades. Is 150 years long enough for the anger to end?

A writer commenting on the 10th anniversary of 9/11 last year raised the question: "Will it ever be possible for us to give up the memory of our wounds? We had better hope so, for all our sakes. And after the commemoration ceremonies are over would be a good time to begin," (Author David Rieff, August 23, 2011 *Christian Century*) There's a subtle difference between forgetting and "giving up the memory." Is it not possible to remember the story so we tell it right and then set aside its power so we can get along?

2. Bad events are easier to remember. Perhaps even more is remembered through the difficult times. The big festivals among the three monotheistic faiths are centered around suffering: Judaism recalls the deliverance from slavery in the Exodus and the wilderness wanderings. Islam observes

the holy time of Ramadan with fasting from food and water from sunup to sundown. Christianity is centered on the inseparable events of Jesus' death and resurrection.

In my mind's eye I can see my great, great grandparents—Andreas and Lena Lundborg, both in their early 50's fleeing for their lives, with their three sons buried at West Lake alongside ten other cousins, nephews, and nieces. The clothes on their back were their only possessions. With them were their oldest son Johannes and his wife, Kristina who was eight months pregnant; their 13-year-old daughter Johanna, and their wounded 9-year-old son Samuel who had been shot in the side and clubbed on the head. In addition they took responsibility for 16-year-old Anna Stina and 7-year-old Peter Broberg, cousins who were the only survivors of the two Broberg households. Walking or in a wagon they journeyed to Paynesville, St. Cloud, Afton, and stopped in St. Paul in the winter because Peter had typhoid fever. They were refugees, the collateral damage of any war, and all they wanted was a safe place, preferably in the company of those who spoke Swedish who would take them in and help them get back on their feet. They found it in Carver County months later. Knowing their suffering, I know more of my family. The memory is painful, but they are revealed.

There was deep suffering among the Dakota. Not all wished to be at war. They were divided concerning how best to meet these settlers who were taking away their land.

In 1983 I met a Dakota man named Eugene Crawford who was raised on the Sisseton Reservation. Gene was a Lutheran who led an organization called the National Indian Lutheran Board, and we were together at a conference to help pastors understand Native American religions. He was a leader and I a participant. One day in a conversation with him I told the story of my relatives—how 13 were killed, and had my great grandfather not survived I would not be here. I was taking a risk. His people killed mine.

He was quiet for a minute. Then he said quietly, "My great grandfather was one of the 38 Dakota hanged for their part in the war." My people killed his.

Here we were—the 4th generation later, both Lutherans, not having to fight about land and identity. We enjoyed one another's company. We returned to our homes, corresponded occasionally, marveled about our connection with each other, and he died three years later. As I've learned more about my great grandfather, I've wondered about Gene's. Books today name the 38 who were hanged. Many authors say the trials and convictions of these men were a mockery. Those who fought the hardest to kill the settlers escaped to Canada, Montana. I learned this past month the name of Gene's great grandfather from a teacher on the Sisseton Reservation. He said Gene's great grandfather had been pardoned by President Lincoln. He never should have been hanged. He said the real question was: was he hanged inadvertently or as an act of retribution? Stories of suffering connect deeply.

The deaths of my relatives were a huge injustice. So was the death of Gene's great grandpa. Knowing our common suffering brought us together.

3. Maybe this is too big a leap, but it seems true to me. We know God through our tough times. I hesitate a bit because the typical faith story is something like this—"Times were tough. I asked for help. God saved me. Life is good." That's grossly oversimplified, but often that's what a Christian witness sounds like. There's usually a hint of victory and triumph.

That was not the experience of my relatives. Times were tough, and then tougher. They were trying to make a new start in a new land hopeful for the best when it all came crashing in upon them. War broke out. Then came the deaths of 13 from their family. They fled. Moved to Carver County. Three years later came back here. Then Lena died at 60, too young, broken heart. Andreas went south again. Lived with one of his sons. No stories of a great epiphany or a moment when everything changed. He hung in there, watched his children marry and give birth. Finally, more than 20 years after his wife's death, at age 78 he died, and the two are buried together at West Union in Carver County. They suffered great loss, coped as well and as long as they could. Sometimes that's all there is.

Where was God? How was God revealed? Reflecting on their lives and the lives of many others I have known over the years I say that God was known in their longings, what they ached for, what they loved and lost, in their broken hearts. In the language of the Apostle Paul longing is found in "groaning—sighs too deep for words" (Romans 8:26) God was in the good memories of days gone by that helped them dream of a day of reunion, of redemption. God was in the remainder of the family where they might have known the gift of mutual consolation. God was in the persistent struggle to get up every morning, to hope for whatever new thing God might be beginning. God was in the hope of heaven. God gave them the gift of yearning.

Life does not always turn out the way we thought it would or should, and many through the centuries have felt the pain of great suffering and loss and have continued to quietly press on. They don't tell triumphant stories, but they cope. They get by. They keep going—often fueled by their longings.

The study of history teaches us to value the past for what we can learn for the present. The stories of suffering need to be told so we don't mindlessly repeat our mistakes. May God somehow help us to learn from the past.

And history tells us there are times when we have to let go of the power of the past—to focus on whatever new thing God might do to bring deliverance. May God help us to not destroy our relationships and our selves by clinging to past hurts.

Where are your longings? You elders, look at the next generations. How does your love for them shape your longings for them? Grace, mercy, peace, love are powerful entities we most notice when they are missing, when we yearn for them, when we long for their return. May the generations to come remember the stories of 1862. May the Dakota and the descendants of the immigrants tell their stories to one another. May there be an outbreak of peace and harmony and reconciliation and healing among the people of all races, colors, and creeds. May that be the new thing God is about to do. May that be our desire, our hope, our longing. May God bless our longings. AMEN.

RESOURCES

❧

A complete bibliography of material available on the 1862 US/Dakota War could be another book all by itself, so here is a modest listing of publications that contain some information about the Brobergs and Lundborgs. Very few books say anything about my relatives, most likely because the majority of the war's pitched battles took place in locations nearer to the Minnesota River.

I must credit other descendants of the survivors who have researched this rich family story. My first cousin, Dr. Richard Lundborg, knew our grandparents well, and as a child he learned much from them. He began to research the family story as a college student and put together a most informative document. He was the first, and he completed his work in the 1980's.

Jack and Carol Lundquist have compiled a thorough genealogy of the descendants of Torsten Algottson. Jack was a descendant of Sarah Lundquist, the daughter of Andreas and Lena who remained in Sweden.

Charles N. Berget, whom I first met August 18, 2012 in Monson Lake State Park, is a great grandson of Anna Stina Broberg, and he has compiled important data about her from family history and valued historical books. These relatives have been generous in sharing their materials.

*Indicates favorites.

Anniversary Album 1859–1944 Lebanon Lutheran Church New London, Minnesota. Published for the Eighty-fifth Anniversary Celebration August 19–20, 1944. It is out of print, hard to find, and accessible only through family members.

If you have one, protect it. It contains photographs of family members.

Breu, Amanda. *The Causes of the Dakota Conflict of 1862*. Self published in 2006 as a senior thesis at the College of St. Benedict in St. Joseph, MN. This resource provides no information on the Brobergs and Lundborgs, but it is easily accessible online, brief (37 pages), well balanced in perspective, and is one of few works willing to address the difficult issue of physical disfigurement practiced by some Dakota on victims. Find it at: www.csbsju.edu/Libraries/Lib-Bib-Award-Winners.htm

Bryant, Charles S. and Murch, Abel B. *A History of the Great Massacre by the Sioux Indians in Minnesota*. Cincinnati, Ohio: Ricky and Carroll Publishers, 1864. It's the 1864 date that makes this book significant. Some have cautioned about sources written too early whose inaccuracies will appear later. This book contains commentary on the "Lomberg" family, which raises questions about its unique observations. But this source contains my first look at a statement made by Anna Stina Broberg when she was 16 years old. At age 81 she wrote an article now more widely known, but this early piece is new to me. Unfortunately, she is named "Ernestina Broburg."

Carley, Kenneth. *The Dakota War of 1862: Minnesota's Other Civil War*. St. Paul, MN: Minnesota Historical Society, 1961, 1976. 100 pages with many pictures, this is an excellent resource for an overview because it is prepared by the Minnesota Historical Society, an organization for which I have much respect. The title and look of the book have evolved over the years, but the content remains dependable. One paragraph summarizes the West Lake Massacre.

Cox, Hank H. *Lincoln and the Sioux Uprising of 1862*. Nashville: Cumberland House, 2005. He's a military historian who describes President Lincoln's quandary dealing with the Civil War and US/Dakota War at the same time. He takes special interest in providing details about Chief Red Middle Voice, a hostile critic of Little Crow, and a chief who specialized in attacking isolated settlers. The book contains slight mention of Lundborgs and Brobergs, and the author must not have had reliable sources.

*Dahlin, Curtis A. *The Dakota Uprising: A Pictorial History.* Edina, MN: Beaver's Pond Press, 2009. I found this to be the best resource of all with great photos and careful research. He mentions our family story and gives evidence he had access to the most reliable histories. This was well worth the $40.

Johnson, Emeroy. *A Church is Planted.* Minneapolis: Land Press, Inc. 1948. Pages 164–181 contain history of the West Lake immigrants with a churchly perspective. The larger story of the book is a history of the beginnings of the Lutheran Minnesota Conference of the Augustana Synod. I'm thankful for this church history text containing an entire chapter on "The Sioux Uprising in 1862."

Johnson, Emeroy. *Eric Norelius: Pioneer Midwest Pastor and Churchman.* Rock Island, Illinois: Augustana Book Concern, 1954. Johnson was a thorough historian of his day, and this account of Norelius' life contains helpful information about the beginnings of the Augustana Synod and Rev. Andrew Jackson's ministry. The archives of the library of Gustavus Adolphus College in St. Peter, MN, include an essay written by Eric Norelius and translated by E. L. Barstow in 1962 about the life and ministry of Rev. Jackson. This essay was helpful to me in understanding Rev. Jackson and his relationship to the Lundborgs and Brobergs.

Lundblad, Larry. "The Impact of Minnesota's Dakota Conflict of 1862 on the Swedish Settlers." *Swedish American History Quarterly.* Rock Island, Illinois: Swedish American Historical Society, July 2000, v. 15, No. 3. Pages 209–221. Lundblad has served as president of Central Lakes College in Brainerd, MN, since 2006. His article is a helpful contribution to family history and sets the Brobergs and Lundborgs in the larger context of other Swedish settlers who had first hand experience of the 1862 war.

Maltmann, Thomas. *Night Birds*. New York: Soho Press, 2007. This historical novel is centered on a German family in southern Minnesota and their experience of the aftermath of the 1862 war. Although it is a fictional account, the author makes use of the story he learned about Andreas Lundborg's gift of a glass of wine to those who helped bury the West Lake victims, and Maltmann integrates it into the plot of his novel without the use of the Lundborg name. I contacted the author to comment on the Lundborg story, and Maltmann said he learned the story from a book he discovered in the archives at Luther Seminary in St. Paul, MN. It must have been Lawson's writings on Kandiyohi County.

*Michno, Gregory F. *Dakota Dawn: The Decisive First Week of the Sioux Uprising, August 17–24, 1862*. New York: Savas Beatie LLC, 2011. Pages 267–291 are all about Kandiyohi County, and Michno's writing contains one of the most thorough accounts of the Broberg/Lundborg tragedy.

Oehler, C. M. *The Great Sioux Uprising*. New York: University Press, 1959. This historical overview was written nearly a century after the war. His book was helpful for his day, but it contains only minimal mention of Brobergs and Lundborgs with skewed details.

Schultz, Duane. *Over the Earth I Come: The Great Sioux Uprising of 1862*. New York: St. Martin's Press, 1992. "History that reads like a novel" was a reviewer's high praise for this overview, but its limited mention of Brobergs and Lundborgs is based on misinformation.

The Centennial History of Kandiyohi County Minnesota 1870–1970. Prepared by Kandiyohi County Historical Society, Willmar, MN: Color Press, 1970. This volume is not easy to obtain. I found my copy online through a Roman Catholic Monastery near Portland, OR. What is most valuable in this publication is Victor Lawson's account of the area's early days through 1905, the year it was published. He is the official historian of Kandiyohi County, born to Swedish immigrants, worked as a journalist, and is buried in the cemetery of Peace Lutheran Church in New London near the monument to the Broberg and Lundborg victims of the 1862 attack. His chapter on "The Massacre at West Lake" was written after but stands alongside Anna Stina Broberg's eyewitness account as the most valuable resources for information on our family's history.

Urdahl, Dean. *Uprising*. St. Cloud, MN: North Star Press, 2007. This historical novel was written by a former high school history teacher from New London. He knows the area and his history, but the Lundborgs and Brobergs make only a brief appearance.

*Wingerd, Mary Lethert. *North Country: The Making of Minnesota*. Minneapolis: University of Minnesota Press, 2010. I found this big new book interesting mostly because of its account of Indian/White relationships dating back to the 1600's. The last two chapters comprising nearly 100 pages describe the buildup to the 1862 war and the war itself. Great illustrations. The book contains no mention of family history, but the author describes the historical context in a most helpful manner.

A Place to Visit and Websites to View

A Center for Swedish Genealogical Studies

Konkordiahuset, a Swedish genealogical center, is the place for the serious student of Swedish family history. It is located in the small village of Hössna in the state of Västergötland. It is owned and operated by Anna-Lena Hultmann, an internationally renowned genealogist, and it includes an upstairs apartment to live in while pursuing studies. The building is a former Swedish Covenant church, and the downstairs is a huge library with many books and computers. Anna-Lena knows her subject matter, is familiar with Swedish church records, and can translate them into English. The location is less than an hour's drive to Vårgårda, the town nearest to where the Lundborgs and Brobergs were born and raised. The churches of Södra Härene, Kullings Skövde, Tumberg, and Algutstorp—churches known to Broberg and Lundborg ancestors—are all in this area. Vårgårda is also where Jerker Saxentorp lives, and he has been the most helpful person in tracking down oral history narratives in the area.

I should note that all of Sweden's church records are available online, so if you are somewhat able to handle the language issue and have the vision and wisdom to decipher odd penmanship, you can learn all you want sitting behind a desk in the comfort of your own home. However, if you lack those skills, check out Anna-Lena's website, www.konkordiahuset.se, and you might want to visit her in Sweden.

Several Other Websites

www.rootsweb.ancestry.com/~mnkandiy/Arctander.htm Ancestry.com is a helpful website for studying genealogy, and this specific page gives information about Arctander Township, which is where the Lundborgs settled. I frequently looked at this site.

www.dakotavictims1862.com/Family_and_Friends_of_Dakota_Uprising/Family_and_Friends_of_Dakota_Uprising_Victims.html Excellent site created this year to observe 150th anniversary of US/Dakota War of 1862. If you have never read the statement Anna Stina Broberg Peterson wrote when she was 81, here is a place to find and read it.

www.usdakotawar.org The Minnesota Historical Society began this site prior to 2012, the Sesquicentennial Anniversary of the Dakota/US War, and viewing it is well worth your time.